INSIDE OUT

EXPLORING THE MENTAL ASPECTS OF DRUMMING

By Billy Ward

Edited by William F. Miller

Design and layout by Joseph C. King

Cover art (in box):
"Wonderwheel" by William Steiger,
www.williamsteiger.com

© Copyright 2003 Modern Drummer Publications, Inc.
International Copyright Secured
All Rights Reserved
Printed In The USA

Any unauthorized duplication of this book
or its contents is a violation of copyright laws.

Published by
Modern Drummer Publications, Inc.
12 Old Bridge Road
Cedar Grove, NJ 07009 USA

DISTRIBUTED BY

Contents

Page

Special Thanks

Every now and then, in the course of one's life, one comes across people who are not only inspirations, but exhibit a friendship and appreciation beyond one's wildest dreams. John Good (vice president of DW Drums) and Bill Miller (editorial director of *Modern Drummer* and editor of this book) fit into this category for me. Because not only did they choose to believe in me when I was too "esoteric" to meet the common standard, but in the process of their courageous championing of me, they graced me by becoming close personal friends and heroes in their own way. Without them, not only would I not have had the chance to have this public forum, but my life would have been poorer for not having them as friends.

I also want to thank my parents, Bill and Gay Ward, who allowed unrestricted drum and band practicing at our house when I was growing up. (The neighbors must have loved that!) Furthermore, they drove me to and from many gigs before I was old enough to drive myself. This incredible physical and emotional support was my foundation, and for this and more, they have my undying love and gratitude.

Until three years ago, writing was just as weird to me as if I'd stepped out from behind a drumkit and started playing guitar. My gratitude extends to the staff at *Modern Drummer* magazine for their encouragement and support in this new path. Jon Albrink, a talented New York City songwriter, guitarist, and bassist, and Maura Robinson, my wife and confidant, offered invaluable perspectives in proofreading many of these articles.

Thanks are also due to my ever-so-supportive manufacturing companies; including DW Drums, Zildjian Cymbals, Evans Drumheads, Shure Microphones, Trueline Drumsticks, as well as Mark Craney, Dave Magee, Doane Perry, and the worldwide "Drum Club." You know who you are. Music is good.

•

Foreword: Thoughts On Billy

The connection between a singer and a drummer is a very mysterious thing. Maybe it has something to do with the physicality involved in both singing and drumming. Or maybe it's the fact that these are the two oldest ways for humans to create music. But the chemistry between a drummer and a singer is in my mind the most important element in creating a band (at least as far as modern popular music goes).

The best drummers I've worked with have lifted me, made my singing feel effortless as breathing, and helped me bypass my conscious mind to get to that non-thinking zone, which is the most fertile place for making music. And I've heard drummers say the same thing about their favorite singers, that a particular voice can energize their playing and make it seem to come from somewhere beyond or above themselves. So the relationship is ultimately very intimate. Choosing a drummer to work with is not unlike choosing a lover. Certain objective criteria may be important (for me a knowledge of blues, soul, and world music styles), but ultimately it's a matter of instinct. You just know when it feels right.

I first saw Billy Ward when he performed with Chris Whitley. Chris was playing music from his *Din Of Ecstasy* album, and Billy was a demon on the drumkit behind him, answering the lightning crackle of Chris's guitar with his own thunderous sounds to make a beautiful storm. I was moved by the fact that Billy seemed to inhabit the songs every bit as intensely as the man who had written them, and even though I had a set road band at the time, I made a mental note about him.

Years later, when I was getting ready to go on the road again, I called Billy. We met at a health food restaurant in Manhattan to discuss the upcoming tour and size each other up. (Because the day-to-day reality of touring is one of forced intimacy, and because you and your band are essentially living together for months at a time, personality is as important a consideration as talent when putting a band together. If you don't get along well with a musician—if he or she doesn't "give good bus"—your tour can be misery.)

I had only spoken to Billy briefly a couple of times and didn't know what to expect from the man who had seemed so intense on stage. We talked for a little while, mostly about the artists he had worked with in the past. And then Billy began explaining a theory he had. Without the slightest hint of irony, he proceeded to tell me that, based on his experience, the more talented singers were, the less *intelligent* they were likely to be.

Joan Osborne

I waited for him to qualify that statement, or to say that I was the exception to the rule, but Billy just gave me a sphinx-like smile—and I started to laugh. I understood that, whether he knew it or not, he was telling me something about his nature. He's a gloves-off kind of person who will say whatever he feels. Billy was telling me that he's a person who would respect me enough not to flatter or manipulate, and who would go boldly in the direction his instincts told him to go even if it meant being dead wrong (which, by the way, he was on that score). If such confidence were paired with inflexibility, it probably would have been overbearing. But Billy seemed just as likely to believe the exact opposite of what he said. And so he got the gig.

Over the course of our working together I've come to realize that this gleeful courage—in combination with great technical skill and a Zen master's appreciation of music's essential abundance—is what makes Billy such an amazing artist. I've read some of the pieces in this book, and I think it won't be long before you know exactly what I'm talking about. I hope some of Billy's gleeful, passionate courage rubs off on you.

Joan Osborne
Recording Artist

In 1944 I was playing drums with the Benny Carter Orchestra. Then one day when we were in Chicago, Benny told me he would have to let me go in order to hire another drummer. After I heard the new man, I decided to give up drumming as a profession; I knew I would never be in the category of my "replacement," Max Roach.

Since those days, I've been fortunate to have in my ensembles and bands unique talents—Max, Tony Williams, Joe Hunt, Jon Christensen, Al Heath, and Lars Bejbom, among others. All of these musicians were capable not only of the drumming fundamentals of keeping time and supporting solos, but they also had the quality of being able to "lift up" the band, acting as a strong undercurrent that propels the music, lending energy and direction.

George Russell

Billy Ward has been a member of my Living Time Orchestra for almost a decade, and I have relied upon him to support the music and musicians, which he has done with artistry and professionalism. Billy leaves his ego off stage (except for the small bit necessary for the challenge), and gives his all. He *listens*, and in doing so responds sensitively to what is going on within the music. He takes chances; he has unflagging energy and enthusiasm and projects positive energy.

In my compositions, I often change tempos several times in as many bars, a challenge especially for the rhythm section. Billy leads the section unflinchingly into each change, and provides "ground support" for the rest of the band. His joy in performance is infectious, and each concert is different, revealing some new element, some fresh idea.

The drummer has great responsibility in any group, and perhaps more than any other chair, possesses the potential to affect the outcome of the performance. Billy has never let me down.

George Russell

Composer, theoretician, bandleader, and innovator George Russell's first book, The Lydian Chromatic Concept Of Tonal Organization *(1953), was the first theory to come from the jazz tradition. It opened the way to modal improvisation, as pioneered in Miles Davis's seminal recording* Kind Of Blue. *Russell has received many awards, including the MacArthur Foundation Fellowship. Russell performs, conducts, records, and teaches throughout the world. For more information, please visit his Web site at www.georgerussell.com.*

Introduction

We all want to get better. But how do we do that? There are fundamentals in drumming such as grip, rudiments, independence, and reading. All these things go into actually playing the drums and, if done properly, not hurting ourselves. To improve on these physical skills, I suggest studying with a teacher. That's what I did. My teachers gave me a solid foundation in the physical skills required for drumming.

Eventually, after working hard on all of the physical skills of drumming, I started playing in bands, experiencing the joy (and trauma) of working with other musicians. Early on in my career, when I wanted to improve at my craft, I worked on things that I already did pretty well. I basically learned to play them faster with trickier variations and greater strength. "Wow, I'm now up to 156 bpm with my double pedals! Surely this stuff will pay off someday."

But for me, this was a lonely grid to pursue. I couldn't find a band that would allow me to showcase how brilliant I was at these heavily practiced techniques. ("If only I could've gotten the gig with The Who, Miles Davis, P-Funk, or....)

Paul La Raia

As I've gotten older and more experienced, I've learned that there are at least two aspects of making music. There's the technical side of being able to actually perform the notes. But there's also the creative—or artistic—side that chooses which notes are best for that moment. I believe the creative side needs to be studied and developed just as intensely as the physical side.

My favorite drummers are simply great *musicians* who happen to play the drums. I don't love them for their accuracy or speed. I love them for their "conversational skills" and the way they make their musical room a better place. And just how does all of this relate to each of us improving at the drums? Whether you're a part-time or full-time drummer, my suggestion is to focus on becoming a better *musician* rather than a better technician. If you do that, your drumming will really improve.

I believe that most artistic growth is mental—or even spiritual. For example, when you play, are you a giver or a taker? Are you saying, "Look at me, look at me"? I think drumming encompasses listening to yourself, but still keeping most of your attention on the entire piece of music you're playing. It's like having a great conversation with your best friend. You're focused on them more than yourself. So, are you the best friend of your band, willing to forgive—and even *hide*—your bandmates' shortcomings?

In the end, it's about love. With love, all the other things are possible—respect, admiration, maybe even money. (But don't count on that in this business.) To truly love, you must first be truthful about yourself. Be honest about your commitment and your abilities. Without truthfulness, you'll achieve nothing. This is why you should record your drumming at every opportunity and listen to it. Judge it harshly, as a stranger would. Then improve your shortcomings.

It might also be wise for you to go back and listen to styles of music you may have previously snubbed. For some, this means opening up to jazz. For others, it might mean opening up to rock or even rap music. It's good to consider all styles, and then develop personal tastes that you've chosen through wisdom and experience, rather than ignorance.

This book is a compilation of articles that I've written for *Modern Drummer* magazine. The first essay started as a diary entry on my Web page and, much to my delight, the editors at *MD* asked to publish it. Many articles have since been published in the magazine, and I've received great joy at the feeling that I've connected with drummers who, like me, want to become better but aren't sure how to do it.

This group of essays pursues some ideas that may provoke some thought, or at least lend you a crowbar toward finding some improvement. (My Quickie Chart System, at the end of this book, is a hell of a crowbar when you're in several bands at the same time.) But your growth starts with you. You must study music and even human nature to become a better drummer. Think. Analyze. You can do it. We drummers are smart.

Music is one of those wonderful gifts of life that shows us a universe that is bigger than us all. Please take these ideas and expand on them. Come up with your own ideas and build a new foundation of truth for yourself.

Thanks,

Billy Ward

Chapter 1

Billy Ward's
Stroke Of Genius

by William F. Miller
(Excerpted from the July 1999 issue of *Modern Drummer* magazine.)

That Billy Ward isn't a household-name drummer is a shame. Talk about "talent deserving wider recognition." In a drumming world filled with highly touted so-so players, Ward is a certifiable monster—impressive chops, an incredibly solid feel, a vast knowledge of styles, and a true sense of touch (practically a lost art these days). Oh, and be sure to include Billy's playful, gregarious personality on that list; it adds a sparkle to any music he touches.

Watching Ward play is simply a treat. Sitting across from the man in his New York project studio, DrumPike, where he spends most of his time adding drum and percussion tracks to various LA and Nashville sides, you can't help but be impressed. Radically diverse images merge and then slap you upside the head when Billy's behind the kit: Purdie's soul-brother swagger, Bonham's bombast, a hint of Zigaboo Modeliste's slipperiness, the down-home honesty of Levon Helm, and, believe it or not, a good dose of Elvin Jones' magical touch and relentless pulse. Ward deals these influences

with the savvy of a master cardsharp.

Billy's ability to astutely balance the creative with the tried-and-true has made him very employable. And the calls come from a broad, head-scratching spectrum: Joan Osborne, Robbie Robertson, Carly Simon, Bill Evans, Richard Marx, George Russell, Ace Frehley— even Yoko Ono! Soundtrack work for Ward has also been plentiful, and the drummer has added his flare for the dramatic to such flicks as Tom Hanks' *That Thing You Do*, Steven Seagal's *Under Siege*, and Whoopi Goldberg's *Sister Act*.

All that work might provide a good living for a pro, but it doesn't necessarily satisfy one's creative soul.... Enter *Two Hands Clapping*, the brilliant, self-produced album featuring Ward sparring one-on-one with heavyweights Bill Champlin, John Patitucci, Joy Askew, Glen Phillips, Jim Beard, and Chris Whitley. Here's where Billy's twenty years' worth of carefully governed pro experience erupts; here's where the man gets to *play*.

Paul La Raia

"I would venture to say that almost any drummer would become the **hottest** player on the planet if he got into his tone enough."

WFM: In this day and age, when so many drummers are obsessed with developing—and *displaying*—chops, listening to you play is a pleasure: You have such a beautiful touch on the instrument.

BW: Thanks, but you can't really blame drummers: We all focus on technique, especially when we're coming up. I do think it's sad that drum teachers don't focus more on touch and tone, though. A beginning trumpet player is taught the importance of tone from the start; it's considered part of the instrument. Why isn't that the case with drums? I think that's part of the reason why there are so many drummers out there who are focused on developing more dexterity as opposed to being better *musicians*.

WFM: Did you have teachers early on who covered the musical stuff?

BW: Not really, although I had a great fundamental background from a local drummer in Cincinnati—where I grew up—named Jack Volk. He taught me the rudiments, rhythmic patterns, the Chapin book—all the basics. And he got me off to a good start, because I was playing in bands by the time I was in sixth grade. But basically I was just your normal schmuck drummer. I had plenty of facility but didn't know anything about touch, groove, or taste.

WFM: What finally made you aware of these things?

BW: I don't think I was aware of touch until I really started listening to jazz, around seventh or eighth grade. First it was Joe Morello with Dave Brubeck, then Coltrane's *My Favorite Things* with Elvin. *Miles Smiles* was my first Miles record. And then I discovered people like Sun Ra and Ornette Coleman—oh, and Mel Lewis. Once you start hearing people like Mel, Blakey, and Elvin, and you hear those incredible sounds, you have to go "duh." I

Paul La Raia

once read a great quote from Art Blakey: "I hear violins in my cymbals." That says so much.

So I started to be aware of touch and tone, but at that point I thought it had something to do with the gear. I became very obsessive about tuning drums and finding the right cymbals. In high school I bought a small Gretsch set after seeing an Alan Dawson clinic. I wanted that sound.

WFM: When did you realize it was something more than the gear?

BW: Not until I was in college. I went to the Conservatory of Music in Cincinnati for a year and a half, mainly to keep from going to Vietnam. It was easy for me because that's where I'm from and I was lucky enough to receive a scholarship. Plus it meant I could stay in town and keep playing in my local rock band.

So I went to the Conservatory, which had a program that was a lot like Juilliard: They didn't have any jazz studies program. But I was up front with them: "I'm going to play jazz." And they said, "Oh yeah, practice the marimba." I loved playing marimba, but honestly, I just sucked at it. And I really hated performing classical music. I just can't count three hundred measures and then play one triangle note. And the stress involved with that...it just wasn't fun. I absolutely *love* listening to that music and I find it very inspiring, but participating in it didn't give me that soaring feeling I got from playing drumset.

While I was at the Conservatory, I had a teacher, Ed Wuebold, who was in the Cincinnati Symphony. *He* was really into tone, and he felt it was his duty to train me. He was like, "I know you're a jazz guy, but I don't know anything about it. You're on your own

there. But I'm going to teach you what I *do* know. Today's lesson: tambourine." So I studied the legit stuff with him.

When we got to working on timpani, things got interesting for me. There's a guy named Fred Hinger, who I don't know, but who was a concert timpanist and had a small mallet company—Hinger Touch Tone, I think it was

Paul La Raia

called. Eddie Wuebold knew of Hinger's technique and taught it to me. Some of these things were pretty out: Eddie had me bouncing tennis balls off the top of the timpani so that I could learn about getting a sound out of a drum!

Paul La Raia

We worked on the Hinger timpani grip, which is where you kind of roll the stick over the top joint of your index finger and everything kind of pivots around that. Working on that really helped my stroke. I know it's given me the ability to play really loud with small sticks. I can also dig in and it's totally comfortable. There's no stress in my hands.

WFM: Watching you play, you do have a very relaxed, loose grip.

BW: That's something I focus on. When you tense up to play, everything sounds bad. Staying loose is one of the keys to getting a good sound. And if you think that by really gripping down hard you'll be able to play fast—forget it. When I play a single-stroke roll, it's the most soothing thing in the world. You'll see some guys with their eyes bugging out of their heads and muscles burning. You can only go so fast doing it that way, and it doesn't sound as good.

It's funny, I don't practice a lot anymore, but when I feel like I do need to practice, I always start with single-stroke rolls. And I don't do it to work on playing fast. I do it to get the roll to feel lovely and to have it sound smooth. Then I'll play the roll on every drum on the kit. When it's sounding good, then I know my playing is pretty close to where it should be. Then I start groovin'…and when I stumble, I stop and work on what caused me to stumble.

WFM: Let's get back to the drumset for a minute, specifically your interest in being a jazz drummer.

BW: I wanted to play jazz fairly early on. And what really hooked me was a lesson I had with Elvin Jones. I was seventeen.

WFM: How did that come about?

BW: I came to New York to buy my first set of Ks. I had met Mel Lewis at a concert he gave near my hometown, and he told me, "If you want decent Ks, you've got to go to New York, to Ippolito's drum shop." So I went to New York, to Ippolito's, and there, just hanging out, was Papa Jo Jones! He was a bit cantankerous, but he helped me pick out my first set of Ks! Then Frank Ippolito said, "Do you want to have a lesson? We have Tony Williams and Elvin Jones available." And I must have looked at him, just mesmerized: "Duh, I want Tony." But then it occurred to me: I really know Tony. I can't do what he does, but I understand it. I don't understand Elvin at all. So I asked for Elvin instead.

That lesson with Elvin changed my life. We were upstairs in a little room and he was on a practice set—these cheap, beat-up drums with terrible cymbals. But when he played that set he sounded just as good as he did on any Trane record. All of those sounds were *right there*. The sound was inside of him, not in the gear he was playing.

WFM: And your fate was sealed....

BW: Oh yeah. I wanted to be Elvin. I played like him for years. That's pretty egocentric to think that you can sound like Elvin, but I know that as a jazz drummer that's what people said about me: "Ah, he sounds like Elvin." I do a pretty good Elvin impersonation on the drums. Of course, I don't have his touch—those huge hands, that magical thing he has. And talk about a loose grip: You wonder how *he* holds onto the sticks!

WFM: It seems like the concept of touch was important to you pretty early on. You mentioned about how it developed from your classical training. Is that something you'd recommend other people investigate?

BW: Honestly, if I hadn't been trapped in music school I would never have practiced it or had the patience to deal with it. I'm glad I did. But I want to make the point that studying classical percussion isn't the only way to develop touch on the instrument. It's like all the different religions—I think there are a lot of different ways to get to the Sun.

The important thing for drummers to learn is how to use their ears. Do you hear *music* in your drums? When you're playing a roll, do you hear *zzzzz*, like a violin? Do you hear it as a long note? Do you think about the duration of the notes you're playing? If you're thinking, whole note on a floor tom, do you play it as a whole note, or do you actually play a quarter note with three quarter-note rests? Developing a sensitivity to touch and tone is largely psychological.

WFM: Do you have any practical tips for drummers wanting to improve their sound on the instrument?

BW: Always record yourself. Don't play anywhere without making a tape. And I think it's *imperative* that you record yourself at gigs. You need that recording to be able to go back and hear what you made the audience and bandmates sit through! I'm sorry, the tape doesn't lie.

So many times I've played what I thought was a burning gig, but then after reviewing the tapes, it wasn't so hot. And there have been times when I thought I was so bad and flat, yet on the tape the performance sparkles. Recording yourself is a great way to monitor what's going on in your playing.

Drummers should also listen to other drummers very carefully—really pick apart what they're doing. Say you want to have a feel like Kenny Aronoff. Well, you have to develop the ears to recognize exactly how he's playing his hi-hat, kick drum, and snare drum when he's playing a groove. And then, after you've got the ears, at least then you know what your goal is. Hopefully then you can begin to hear how close you are.

Billy's Kit

Drums: DW in red sunburst/zebra wood finish
A. 5x13 aluminum snare
B. 8x12 tom
C. 13x15 floor tom (with legs)
D. 12x20 bass drum
E. 8x28 Woofer

Cymbals: Zildjian
1. 10" hi-hats (Special Recording Series, with tambourine jingles on bottom cymbal)
2. 18" crash (A Custom or K Constantinople)
3. 20" A Zildjian & Cie Vintage ride mounted X-Hat style over a 14" EFX Piggyback China

Hardware: DW, including a three-legged hi-hat stand and a Turbo sprocket double pedal (spring tension on main pedal is set tight as possible, left pedal has a medium tension and is positioned "outside"—to the left of—the hi-hat pedal)

Heads: Evans coated G2 on snare batter, Hazy 300 snare-side head (no muffling, medium tension top and bottom), coated G2s on tops of toms with clear G1s on bottoms (no muffling, medium tension), EMAD bass drum batter with EQ3 Resonant on front (Evans pillow for bass drum muffling)

Sticks: Trueline Billy Ward model (similar to their TG Rock and TG Jazz models, but with a rounded tip)

Percussion: Rhythm Tech Hat Trick (brass jingles), Canz shakers

Microphones: Shure Beta 91, SM81, Beta 52, Beta 57, and KSM-44

Electronics: Geoffrey Daking mic' pre's, limiters, and console

---

Developing a sense of touch and pulling a good tone from your instrument all boils down to wanting it and hearing it. The world is big. Everybody doesn't have to be obsessed with having greater speed or dexterity. Sure, you can be in a band that wants a lot of double bass drumming. Some people love it; when I'm in a certain mood *I* love it. You can develop those chops and go there. But you know, look at Ringo, man. What a great sound! How about Jim Keltner, Billy Higgins, or Levon Helm? These are guys who know how to get a great sound out of their drums.

WFM: So you'd say being a good drummer has more to do with the sound you produce than the notes you play?

BW: Absolutely. I would venture to say that almost any drummer would become the hottest player on the planet if he got into his tone enough. Because when you get there it leads to being more musical, and being more musical leads to more people enjoying playing with you, and that leads to more and more gigs.

WFM: So *that's* your secret to success.

BW: Well, I don't feel I'm that big of a success. I wish I'd figured this stuff out a long time ago.

WFM: What finally turned the light bulb on?

BW: For me, honestly, I think it was having my private life safe and secure, feeling in love and happy. I needed to get to a place where I was able to relax, where I didn't feel like I had to prove anything, and just get back to what means the most to me.

I've always had this battle: For some reason, I've always been able to have quite a bit of chops. I used to practice like a maniac—but I did back off a bit when I was around twenty-one because I realized that I didn't want to become some freak who couldn't play with anybody.

WFM: There are a few drummers today who seem to be practicing for drum clinic performances and not for gigs.

BW: I have nothing against those types of players. I totally respect the effort they put into it. But the question I asked myself was, Do you want to be a star drummer or do you want to play music?

WFM: Even with all of your years in the business, you still seem very positive about music, very energetic.

BW: When I'm working on a project I'm very exuberant and hyper. And when I'm excited about something I can't be held back.

WFM: That's probably a reason why people hire you.

BW: It's also a reason some people *don't* hire me. A lot of times people like it if you're just a little more gray. I get excited, I want to get into the music, I want to bring a lot to it. Some people want you to come in and just do the job—lay down the track and go home. I can certainly try to do that, but it's not satisfying.

WFM: I'd think a producer or artist would want musicians who play from the heart.

BW: You have to watch that, though. You have to balance the highs and the lows. I'll tell you, I've had to work very hard at controlling myself on a gig. I'd be up there, the music would be soaring, and *bam*, I'd get so excited that I'd launch into some outlandish fill. It would be coming from a place of total joy, but it might not be appropriate. I had to learn to control that.

I think the people who hire me know what I'm about. I tend to work with slightly stranger artists, people who are incredibly tal-ented but who go their own way—you know, like Robbie Robertson, Yoko Ono, Jimmy Webb. When I work with more normal people, *I'm* not as satisfied. I love it when I'm recording with an artist and they say, "Billy, I really want *you*. I want your magic. If you feel like doing something, just do it."

WFM: Let's talk a bit more about keeping control of your emotions when you play. You mentioned getting excited and ruining "the moment" by overplaying. How did you learn to control that?

BW: I actually found a new way to think about it from baseball. I'm a baseball freak; I love baseball's intangibles and the Zen qualities of the game. Tom Seaver, not only one of the greatest pitchers of all time but also one of the most intellectual, had a term for controlling one's emotions: "staying inside yourself." If he got worked up and threw a fastball as hard as he possibly could, what would happen is the ball would kind of die and not move as fast. Hitters would be all over it. But when he stayed inside himself, in other words staying inside his mechanics, even if he was in front of 60,000 people, he would keep his composure. I love that kind of psychological mindset.

I mentioned earlier about a lesson I had with Elvin. He's *way* into the mental aspects of drumming. I remember asking him why sometimes I would play well and other times I would just suck. He called it "I thoughts." In other words, if you're playing and any sentence that starts with "I" comes into your head, like "I'm doing great" or "I'm going to play a fill here," you're in trouble. Elvin told me that if you're thinking that way, you're not playing for the music. I'll never forget that.

•

Chapter 2

Drums Are **Musical** Instruments

Some people in the neighborhood where I live in New York go to the gym every day. Their bodies are extremely pumped up, yet they don't plan on doing any sports—at least not baseball, basketball, football, or stuff like that. They go to the gym just to feel good about themselves. Other people work out so that they can excel at a particular sport.

I think there are some drummers who practice like this. Some go into their practice room and work on some difficult fill or rhythm, seemingly doing it for their own benefit—just for the feeling of personal accomplishment. Other drummers practice things that will help them with their band.

Would you rather have a Super Bowl ring, or do you want to lead all the other quarterbacks in the league with the lowest interception ratio? Did you just play that double bass drum fill because it felt good to display what you've been practicing (your new muscles)? Or did the song really call for it?

When we practice the drums (or work out), endorphins are released. We get a groovy "high"—and a sense of accomplishment. Ever wonder why, when we play in our band, that same wonderful feeling doesn't happen? Maybe we're simply not playing right. Or maybe it's because we're not *practicing* right.

Whether you're practicing *or* performing, ask yourself one question: Am I playing for my vanity and personal benefit, or am I a team player? I admit, this is a very "black and white" way to look at this subject, but it at least encourages some thought, doesn't it?

Honestly, I'm not knocking either approach. But personally, I believe there is far more joy in playing for the song. It gives me a deeper satisfaction when I've helped everyone else in the band feel good. One of my favorite guitar players *is* my favorite because of how he makes *me* feel. His feel and time are so great that he makes me feel invincible. That's the kind of influence I'd like to aim for when I'm playing with people.

Paul La Raia

"Drums **are** musical! We knew that when we were little kids playing on pots and pans."

This is my advice: If you want to practice to have faster feet, please *stop practicing on your instrument*. Work on speed and coordination on pads. Whenever you sit at the drums, play music. Make it a habit. Don't forget, we all play what we practice—and we should be practicing what we play. Drums *are* musical! We knew that when we were little kids playing on pots and pans. Now that we have these fancy instruments, let's not forget it.

Here's a simple exercise to try to get you to think more musically (and less technically) on the drums: Let's call it "Drums I-Ching." It's kind of a musical version of starting a boy scout fire in the forest with two sticks. Here's what you do: The next time you sit down at your drums, drop your sticks on the drumkit. That's right, just drop 'em! You can do this by literally letting go of your sticks, or you can just empty your head and let your hands fall onto the drums or cymbals. Listen to the sounds that creates. The first three sounds that you hear are your assigned motif. Let's say the three sounds were a click from a tom rim (along with a faint hum of the head vibrating), a tom sound, and a snare sound. Okay, these are going to be the three notes of your motif. Beethoven wrote his entire fifth symphony based on two sounds—intervals of thirds. I'm pretty sure we can play a five-minute drum piece based on three sounds.

Now, the moment you hear these three sounds, notice the pitches and notice their relationship in pitch volume (dynamics) to each other. Please understand, you're allowed to use the whole kit in this solo piece. Just keep the three sounds as the compositional center of your statement. If you don't know how to proceed, then you're thinking too much. Empty your drummer-brain. Let that creative jazzy-or-symphonic dude that lives inside of you come out for a little while. (If this isn't working for you, give a listen to Stravinski's "Firebird Suite" or Tom Waits' *Bone Machine* album for inspiration.) Try it—you might love it! This has been a part of my practice for more than twenty years.

Another related exercise: How many sounds can you get out of *each* piece of your drumset? You probably have heard the story of Papa Jo Jones playing at a drum festival and coming out with only a hi-hat—and absolutely *killing* everyone with what he played on it. How about the above Drums I-Ching exercise with one object? Your snare…your hi-hat…your tom-tom…your dog?

The odds are that you (like me) won't play anything that you'd necessarily want someone to hear. But these little private musical moments with your instrument might open your ears, quiet your brain, and teach you how to play more from the heart. Don't just practice technique, practice *music*.

How Do You Get **Gigs**?

New-Age Answers For An Age-Old Question

Vamp

How do you get work? Wow. The most obvious answer—and what has happened with me most of the time—is someone has "championed" me. That is, another musician who knows of a gig has recommended me. But that's so *passive*. I mean, you can't control when such a recommendation will come along. What if you need a gig *now* because you've got bills? What are *you* going to do?

Verse

Fifteen years ago I spent a bit of time hanging out at nightclubs with the Mick & Keith types, figuring (hoping) that this would get me work. Some people have success with the hanging out thing. In my case, it was a complete waste of time. In retrospect, I think my father's advice was relatively accurate: Who we hang out with reflects who we are as people. But translating this into a gig? I really don't know. Now, as I'm raging through my middle years, I've figured a few things out for getting gigs that at least work for me.

I have to thank my friend (long-time Jethro Tull drummer) Doane Perry for one suggestion that has been very helpful. Some years ago, when I was depressed about my work options, Doane said, "Billy, when you want to get a call for a gig, just go and play your drums." He didn't say practice, he said *play*. Make music! All by yourself! For some reason, doing this places a power into the universe (or whatever label you want to give it), and calls start to come. It always seems to work.

There is a trick to this, though. You have to follow up on the calls that *do* come—be they for a gig, a jam session, an audition, whatever. Even if it's a gig with some bad country dude or some crummy Eminem-ish rap thing that

"You don't want to tell the universe that you're not interested in what it has offered you— that's **bad** juju!"

you hate the most. Whatever it is, just do it. It will be good for you. Besides, you don't want to tell the universe that you're not interested in what it has offered you—that's bad juju!

Chorus

Now for the hard part. What should you work on in your playing to get those calls to come? Believe me, I know how hard it is to get inspired and play music when depression takes over. But that's what's so great about music. It's like a mountain lake: As soon as you jump into the water, it refreshes you and fills you with creativity (and hope) again.

When I'm alone in my studio and I don't know what to play, I noodle on the drums until something inspires me. Then I let myself be taken away into that cool, creative space. I try *never* to play the drums without looking for those good/creative/ inspiring moments. You can do this when you practice by practicing looking for the moment.

When you get inside that moment, you're being creative and enjoying your own uniqueness. Pay attention to everything that you're playing when these special moments occur. If you're grooving and feeling like maybe you're inside of something good—and then you mess up—that's totally cool! *Now* you know what you need to work on! You just messed up something that belongs to *you*, so practice that and get it together. Good job!

Bridge

Now I've wandered away from the subject of getting a gig—and the car payment is due! Okay, here's an idea that will help you get work *and* make you a better musician: Get inspired by non-drummer musicians. Are you "into" bass players enough to have an involved discussion with a bass player about Charlie Haden...Rick Danko... Geddy Lee...Lee Sklar? Whoever!

If you can get into another instrumentalist's world enough to really sympathize with his or her musical orbit, then at least two really cool things will happen: 1) That instrumentalist will love you for being so aware of his world. (This will probably make you his favorite drummer.) And 2)—this one's even better—You'll truly become a better drummer. If we can each learn in our own way the things that made Jimi Hendrix or Miles Davis great, we'll apply those creative principles to *our* music. We'll become better musicians, i.e. better drummers!

Final Chorus

Two real-life examples for you: Back in the mid-1980s I went to a Jaco Pastorius bass clinic. While there I met saxophonist Bill Evans. From that meeting we ended up working together for a couple of years. In Bill's band I played with tremendously talented musicians like Jim Beard, Jon Herrington, and Victor Bailey. It was wonderful. (Thanks, Bill!) But it all started with me going to a bass clinic!

The next example involves being open to playing with somebody new, somebody you're not familiar with. After performing at the Modern Drummer Festival in 2000, I was feeling a bit blue. Once again I felt like I needed a shot in the arm regarding playing. (It's easy to get stuck in a rut when most of your work is in the studio.) I decided to dedicate twenty minutes or so (it doesn't take much), whenever I could, to playing some *music* on my drums. I also told several friends (non-musician friends, by the way) that I was looking for something new.

Well, I received an email through my Web site about a band needing a drummer. These guys weren't an established act, but after checking out their music I found it to be really interesting. They needed a drummer to showcase for a record deal. I knew they wouldn't have any money to pay me (until they got their deal), and they probably wouldn't want me to be their regular drummer. They were a lot younger, and I'm probably over-qualified (maybe too much of a smarty-pants?) for them. But I didn't want to turn down what the Universe had given me.

I took the subway out of Manhattan to Brooklyn on a hot, muggy day and, in a dark, dirty, funky studio, I auditioned for the gig. I had fun playing with the band, and it was a

new experience. I wish I could tell you how it turned out, but I don't know. They haven't called me! I seriously doubted they would have asked me to play in their band, and if they did, I probably couldn't have done it anyway. But I made two new friends, and I got to play something different.

The point is, since I went to that audition, the universe has been good to me. I received a call to play on a major tour.

From all of this, though, I *know* that there are other wonderful things out there for me—floating...hovering...waiting. These "definite possible maybes" could all pass away into a vapor, leaving me still looking for more work. But I'd like to believe that I started something by playing my drums for twenty minutes.

Outro

Before I finish, I'd like to be clear that I am not the most happenin' drummer in the world. Most of the time, I know how badly I'm playing. But I stay aware, and I try to stay honest.

In baseball they tell you to "keep your eye on the ball." It sounds simple, like some of the things I've mentioned here. In fact, there's really no reason that you should try my "getting a gig" advice unless you feel like it. Let's face it, I never got to play with Miles Davis. But I've got my "eye on the ball." Do you?

Learning To **Groove**
Being Musical Is The Key

I've been receiving emails from many of you asking about how to groove more. So I thought I'd throw a few ideas out there that you can take to your drumset.

For starters, listen to the *sound* of the drums played by your favorite drummers. Don't pass this wonderful sound off by saying, "Well, that sound is coming from the way it was recorded," or, "That drummer has better equipment than I do and that's why he sounds better." Take responsibility for your sound! Try to figure out how to do it. Tape-record yourself for proof. In my opinion, spending an entire afternoon trying to tune one drum can be time well spent.

Another thing to keep in mind about your groove is how you "voice" what you play. (Voice = tones, dynamics, and interactions between the drums and cymbals.) The way we voice our kit greatly affects our sound, musicality, and feel. Need proof? Go into your CD collection and find a drum beat that your favorite drummer played. Program this beat into a drum machine with all velocity (volume) settings at "normal." Give it a listen: The groove doesn't feel all that good, does it? Now, change the volume/velocity of the hi-hat pattern. That helps. Do the same with the bass drum and snare drum and things improve even more. Adjust the volume correctly, and the machine becomes more human. That same concept can help your drumming feel better. For example, snare drum backbeats are usually twice as loud as the hi-hat. And the hi-hat has its own unique dynamics. Use your ears!

When drum machines were peaking in popularity, I was once hired to program a Bernard Purdie–style beat for a song. It took me four hours to get all the ghost notes just right, and it was really frustrating to figure out how to do it. But in the end I had learned great details about the Purdie magic, and I was able to translate it into my own playing.

Paul La Raia

"I tend to appreciate the **colors** a drummer has chosen more than the particular right-hand/left-hand beat he or she is playing."

Don't have a drum machine? Totally *not* important. It's being able to play that counts, right? When you play that favorite beat of yours, tape-record yourself. It's okay if all you have is a crummy Walkman or whatever. All you need is to be able to hear what's going on, so that you can make the necessary adjustments to groove on that beat just as much as your favorite drummer does.

Listen to the tape. The hi-hat was too loud. Okay, record again with more of a "dance" inside the hi-hat pattern. Now, can you make the groove feel the same by playing brushes? Can you play it on just a snare drum and nothing else? You should be able to. When you *own* a groove, you can play it on your leg!

When you're learning a song, be aware of the dynamic (volume) shape of the song. Is it muscular? Is it restrained? Is it aggressive? Is it slinky? On some songs the drums are an impartial witness—they're driving on cruise control exactly fifty-five miles an hour. ("Hey Nineteen" by Steely Dan is a good example of this kind of groove.) Maybe it's just the intro and verse that has this fifty-five-mile-per-hour feel, but at the chorus there's a feeling of panting—or even aggression.

What's the attitude of the drummer in the song: Happy? Confident? Moody? The musical colors that the drummer chooses (the sticks, drums, or cymbals used) can set an extreme mood.

The next time you're practicing with your band, play the backbeat with one of those half-stick/half-brush dealies, like Pro-Mark Hot Rods. Keep the drumstick in your "ride" hand and the Rod in the backbeat hand. Notice how the feel and mood changes. Try turning off the snares on your snare drum. (This makes things sound really moody to me.) Or try turning the snares off only on the verse, then turning them on in the chorus if you want it to explode more.

Want more examples? Put a towel over your floor tom and play the hi-hat pattern on that instead of the hi-hat. You can also use a Hot Rod (for more top-end attack), or one of Vic Firth's shaker mallets. (I love those suckers.) Play the rest of the song normally. When the song lifts to the chorus (or the second verse), keep the pattern on the tom-tom, but introduce 8th notes with your hi-hat foot.

Try not playing cymbal crashes at all. (Remember the Peter Gabriel album where Jerry Marotta didn't play cymbals on the whole recording? Thanks, Jerry: U da man.) Or maybe just go to the cymbals at the very end of the tune to blow it up real good. You can lose the towel on the tom near the end as well. This makes your touch on the drum more important to the groove. Bury the mallet or stick into the head to "choke" the tom for certain notes. Find your own way to expand on this theme. Hmmm...*fun*.

Listen to yourself as you play each of these ideas. If you're thinking while you're playing, make the pattern simpler. Don't think! Be an impartial witness. That's the head space you want to have. I'm hoping that at least one of these suggestions will send you away on a musical tangent that lasts for hours.

You're probably beginning to get my thoughts on practicing. But I'm going to say it again: Practice technical things away from the drumset—at least most of the time. Keep the drumset for working on music. Practice rudiments on a pad, electronic drums, or something like the Rhythm Tech LapTop. Reserve the drumset for working on your musical self.

Touch (your tone and your ability to get it) is more important to me than technique (dexterity or speed). I tend to appreciate the *colors* a drummer has chosen more than the particular right-hand/left-hand beat he or she is playing.

I was recently flipping through some television channels here in New York and found Jack DeJohnette playing a drum solo on a jazz channel. I hadn't listened to Jack in a long time, and he sounded great. He seemed to be playing "out of time," but I was noticing and enjoying his colors. He was playing very aggressively, mostly on his three toms. About the time I started to *feel* the tempo inside his solo, the band (including Wayne Shorter) came in. They were playing "Giant Steps" by John Coltrane. The band sounded terrific, but what I mainly came away with from that performance was the impression that the great jazz drummers really know about colors!

I think my own background in jazz is what first tweaked my ears to the pitch and harmony of drumming. In jazz, this is very important. But it's also important in rock 'n' roll. Listen to Buddy Holly's "Peggy Sue," The Rolling Stones' "Paint It Black" (wow, Charlie's tom roll starts the whole thing!), Ringo and The Beatles, Terry Bozzio with Robbie Robertson on "Broken Arrow".... The examples are endless and from every era.

Re-listen to your favorite drummers and see what they're doing with their colors. Art lies in the details, and playing an incredible groove on the drums is about caring for *all* of the details. Use your four limbs, your head, and your heart. Instead of only four colors, try using two hundred. It's all about the little things. So get out that magnifying glass for your ears and get to work!

•

Chapter 5

More On Learning To Groove
Confidence, Consistency, And Count-Offs

"1...2..., 1...2...3...4...." The count-off. On the gig, night to night, giving consistent tempos is one of the more obvious places we drummers can excel. But tempos have to do with time, and we all know that subject is a big bag of worms. (The secret torture of being a drummer—ouch!) But I'm hoping to help you with a few concepts and practical tips that I use to tackle the subject.

When the musicians you're working with aren't too mature or experienced, counting off a good tempo is pretty worthless because nobody's going to stick with it anyway. When you listen to the tapes of your gigs and rehearsals, you will find out if you and your band are in this predicament. If you are individually or collectively having trouble playing in time, then an awareness of the problem and some extra practice needs to happen. But when everyone in the band can play well, all it takes is a proper count-off—*at the perfect tempo*—to make the song come alive.

Time is a very relative thing. Shakespeare, in his play *As You Like It*, talks about how time is different for someone *with* his lover (it flies) compared to someone who is *waiting* for his lover (it crawls). I find that I'm affected by this phenomenon. Sometimes a song feels way slow—and other times fast. Who knows what it really was? You could call this "FUD," which stands for fear, uncertainty, and doubt. FUD's a killer.

Working Out The Bugs

Technology can assist us sometimes. I combat FUD by using a metronome that "memorizes" the tempo of each song in the show. This is a good reality check. If, during the playing of a song, I've worried about the tempo, as soon as it's finished, I check the metronome again to find out if I've shifted. Also, I'll sometimes use The Beat Bug or a Groove Guide (by Drum Perfect) in rehearsals. My Groove Guide sits on my snare drum and measures the time between backbeats. It allows me to check my time while I'm playing a song.

"Sometimes I give it up and move the tempo. But other times I shake my head 'no,' and somehow, due to the band's trust and faith in me, they don't **fire** me on the spot."

This type of device helps me to notice the tempo during that eight-bar bridge that felt great, so that the next time I count off the tune it's exactly at *that* tempo. This really helps in rehearsals or gigs with extremely picky singers or bands.

When I use the Groove Guide, I make a big thing out of it to the band. I make sure they know what it does—that it shows me the tempo any time I look at it. Of course, any question by the band about tempo is allowed. Maybe they want to know if that last song sped up at the end. If it sped up, I apologize and say, "Yes, it sped up. Did it feel better to you at the end at that faster tempo?"

Paul La Raia

Always be truthful. Admitting guilt, taking responsibility, and being open is the first thing that leads to your credibility in the band. (Well, maybe it's the second thing. Playing well would have to be the first.)

I used a Groove Guide in rehearsals with Joan Osborne. I even took it on the road for the first two weeks of shows—not because Joan was paranoid about tempos, but because *I* was! I knew that she knew the right tempos for her music, and I was still learning how her singing/body/heart worked. And she deserves great tempos, so I used all the technology I could for reinforcement.

"The key to finding the best tempo—and remembering it—is finding that particular place in each song that the tempo is **crucial**."

Finding The Key

The key to finding the best tempo—and remembering it—is finding that particular place in each song that the tempo is *crucial*. Maybe it's the bridge after the guitar solo, or the very first verse, or the chorus. Whatever it is, that's the *key* part that I sing to myself to get the click tempo for the next song. Once I have it in mind, I dive into the song as quickly as possible. Why wait around for second thoughts?

I personally prefer to train the band to a one-bar count-off. That way there are no doubts about it. If it's a live gig and they're changing guitars between songs, I ask the guitar player who is making the change to look at me when he's ready. As soon as he looks, I count. The bottom line is, I truly believe that the tempo is up to me. *This is my job, and I run the train*. Try to get everybody used to that idea.

Making Adjustments

I'm running the train…yes I am…I think I am…yes I am…Sam I am…2… 4…2!…4!…feels good. What's that? The *singer* is turning to me *during the show* and *demanding* that I speed the song up! How do we drummers deal with this? Don't *we* run the train? Well, sometimes I do give it up and move the tempo. But other times I

shake my head "no," and somehow, due to the band's trust and faith in me, they don't fire me on the spot. It's hard to get away with this, but when you've established credibility and the band knows how hard you've worked to have the best tempo, they will acquiesce.

Sometimes the band wants it faster simply out of panic. But what the heck, it's only music, ya know? Let them have what they want. Speed the darn thing up!

The really good singer/songwriters have a "tempo memory" that is more rock-solid than almost anything I can cook up. My guess is that good singers have a very real physical memory of their breathing between the words and pitches that gives them a better memory of tempo. This is another reason why I say that we drummers should always take a physical snapshot of our bodies when we're grooving. Good singer/songwriters have their actual human physiology to back up their sense of tempo. That's what *we* need to do.

Get the pace of the song into your body and remember it when the metronome is clicking. I only need two clicks from the metronome to confirm the tempo before I count it off. Since I know my key to the song, I'm feeling the tempo inside *that part* of the song. I'm feeling the physical snapshot of playing it, and I'm ready to dive in and bet the farm on it.

There's something else about singers: They're *always* allowed to change the rules of what the tempo is. (Let's feel sorry for them. They don't have all that cool wood, metal, and hardware around them like we do.) I just try not to let it happen too often on stage. In rehearsal, I say, "Great, let's try it," no matter what I think about the idea. If after the show the singer says, "That was too slow," I say, "Oh, okay. Do you want to play it faster tomorrow night and see how it feels? How much faster? Just a tick or two?"

It's wonderful to let your band or singer know that you're pliable and that you'll not question them or their opinion. I discuss tempos right up front. First day of rehearsal…soundcheck…first take…whatever the situation is. I also try to get the people who play with me to understand that I've spent a really long time working on tempo, and that while I'm not perfect, I am pretty darn consistent.

All that said, let's say your singer turns to you and asks if the tempo was faster that night. Remember what I said earlier: Tell the truth! You'll become credible and trustworthy. So later, as they begin to trust you more, even though they are certain that the tempo was different, when you say it was the same, they'll believe you. They'll just figure it was that cup of coffee before the show that made them feel differently about the tempo. But you've got to be honest at all times!

Feelings

Be aware of your feelings and those of the people around you. During the tour, sometimes Joan Osborne would mention that one song was too fast. I'd have gotten the same feeling. So my reply would be, "I know. I felt that way, too. But

it was the same tempo we've been at for over a week now. Do you want to change the tempo tonight?" Other times she might say that it was too fast even though I knew it was dead-on. Listen to me now, drummers: Never tell a band or a singer that they are *not* feeling something that they say they're feeling. It won't help at all.

Feelings aren't necessarily logical, but they are always real. Don't negate them. At least sympathize—even if you don't agree. My answer when they say the tempo sucked and I know it was right on? "Wow! That's amazing, 'cause I thought it was great." Then maybe I'll say, "Let's listen to the tape of the show and check it out." Or more simply, "Do you want it faster or slower tomorrow night?" Honesty and open discussion will give birth to the most valuable thing a band can possess: *confidence!*

My advice is to first size up the abilities of your band. Give them every credit for the things they're good at, and use their abilities to your advantage. The guitarist's rhythm part feels good on the bridge of the song? Remember that, and when you're playing the bridge, compare that moment with all of the physical snapshots you've taken of all the times it's felt great. The bass player is totally groovin' on the chorus of a particular song? Every time you play that chorus, listen to the bass player and make sure it's all feeling right. These confirmations help keep away the deadly FUD that will inhibit your playing. Then size *yourself* up the same way.

There will be certain grooves or tempos that *you're* better at than others. Count on yourself…lean on yourself…trust in yourself when you're playing those kinds of grooves. Hopefully the bass player owns the grooves that you *don't* own yet, and you can lean into him or her on those songs!

•

Chapter 6

So You Want To Be A **Session** Drummer?

The most important thing you possess in a recording session is your ears. As a producer, I can assure you that you've been *hired* because of your ears, not your hands or feet. Of course, hopefully your hands and feet are your obedient servants.

You should have in your hands, feet, and ears all kinds of grooves to call on for whatever particular session you're doing. I'm not talking about exactly copying what other drummers have played, because that's impossible. We are all unique. But trying to "get in the head" of some of the great players of the past will help you in your quest for a career as a session drummer. (Feel free to imitate from the great performances of the past. When you do it, it'll be yours and will automatically come out *your way*.)

Who should you copy? How about Bernard Purdie? When it comes to session drumming—and playing with feel—he's a big one. You should be able to do a serious Purdie impression. I'm always working on mine, because his grooves are sexy. And little bits of Purdie will help your feel in many ways.

Who else do you need in your musical suitcase? Keith Moon! Can you play "My Generation" or "Substitute" with his wild abandon? How about Charlie Watts' "I don't really care" feel? Have you explored drummers like Ringo Starr and Jim Keltner—how they might ride on a tom-tom instead of a cymbal? Do you try that at your rehearsals in the verse, pre-chorus, or chorus of a song?

With the recent (and very controversial) Ken Burns TV series, this is a good time to study the art of jazz and get as much of it into your heart as you can. Buy some records. It's like studying with the best! Do you know Art Blakey and the finality and commitment of his grooves? Do you *hear* Elvin Jones? Genius. He's a dragon back there; he flies and spits fire benevolently. Tony Williams? More fire—and colors. Max Roach? He played *songs* on his drums with his hands…brushes…whatever! Go way back and check out Baby Dodds. If Baby Dodds had been around in the '70s, I think he'd have been John Bonham! (To help you get started, notice that in jazz the ride cymbal pattern and hi-hat are what the snare and bass drum are in rock.)

My point is this: To have a successful career as a session player, knowing different players and styles is important. And knowing *extreme* styles can be like spices in cooking. A little turmeric can go a long way, but it's great when you're making an Indian curry. This knowledge can add a subtle undertow to your groove.

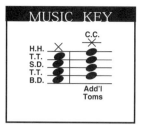

MUSIC KEY

Fills

Each of us has our favorite drummers' performances. For me, these performances are attached to the songs they played. I always loved Nigel Olsson's rock-ballad fills—but how can I separate those fills from the great Elton John songs in which they appeared? To love a drum fill without understanding why it works so well in that particular song is missing the lesson. Let me put it this way: Fills are to drummers what guitar solos can be to guitar players. How many times have you wished your guitar player would just *shut up* and play rhythm? We drummers can be just as hurtful.

At a session for an album that I played on by a wonderful songwriter named Marc Jordan (*Cow*, on RCA), producer Kim Bullard took me aside and told me he had a specific rule about drum fills as a result of years he'd spent programming drums: "Always flow out of the fill into the next section unless there's a specific musical reason not to."

I was totally not ready to listen to a keyboard-playing producer tell *me* what to play, but this made sense. I had always thought of fills as *my moment*, the time to prove that I'm a good drummer. ("This one'll kill 'em. Hah!") Obviously, I really had no clue. Since then, I've learned that fills are no different from anything else in music—just another moment in time (pun intended). No more, no less.

What does it mean to flow into the next section? To help explain what a "flowing fill" is, I need to first show a non-flowing fill. First the time pattern, and then the fill:

This fill could work, and *does* work in certain situations. But it does create a sort of stopping point in the music. It's kind of like a diver jumping on a diving board on beat "4."

Now let's slightly change the fill and make it flow to the next section. Here are a few ideas:

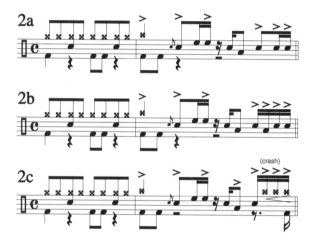

In example 2c, the cymbals are playing the same rhythm that the drums played in 2b, with a little bass drum support added to help go to the next section. (Yes, we can use our cymbals in a fill just as we use the toms. The cymbals simply take up less space, but still move things along.)

The possibilities are endless in how we fill. I hope that the fills you choose to play have something to do with the vocal rhythm, the bass line, the melody—something that *already* exists in the song.

Is a fill's purpose to lift smoothly, even invisibly, into the next section of the song? If so, then sometimes just an *accent* will do the job perfectly.

Just adding that accent on the hat at the end can be all that's necessary. Can you say "Charlie Watts"?

"Knowing different styles is important. Knowing **extreme** styles is like spices in cooking."

You can *remove* something—even from this simple beat—and it will serve as a fill. (Notice the omitted bass drum note on beat 3.) Ah, subtlety.

Here are a few more examples based on the previous, simple Charlie Watts–like fill. This is actually more what Charlie would *really* do:

I play fills like these next two all the time, because they don't use a lot of notes, they feel great, *and* they flow.

Or

The above two fills could be used in a softer song by substituting the hi-hat (closed or open) for snare or tom hits.

Do I play a flowing fill every time I fill? Heck no! Sometimes we need to put a stop on things— a button. And some fills are big dramatic "sign posts" that announce boldly, "Here it comes, fasten your seat belts!" Some music calls for this kind of drama. Film scores are where you might find these. When the bad guy is finally getting killed: "I hate you, I hate you, I hate you!" Or heart-wrenching ballads: "I love you so much I'm gonna diiiieeee!"

Examples of these types of dramatic fills are hardly necessary, because we all play them easily. But here's one that we all probably know: Phil Collins' tom fill in "In The Air Tonight." Now *there's* a musical announcement.

Determining the nature of a song is a distinction that we, as drummers, need to make to play the song *at all*. This totally affects our fills. What is the essence of the song? When in doubt, I always automatically default to smooth, flowing fills.

Finally, the thing that needs to be repeated over and over again is, if you want to be a great musician and have a career as a session drummer, *listen* to music. Listen to a whole bunch of it and understand what you're hearing. Know a song's form: the verse, the pre-chorus, the chorus, the second verse, the bridge. Tape yourself as often as possible, and make yourself listen to it as critically as possible. (Put yourself through what you're putting your bandmates through!) Also, listen to non-drummers, great musicians like George Shearing, John Lennon, Glenn Gould, Patsy Cline. Even if it's music you don't dig, things can be learned.

One more thing: I work hard at keeping my ears open. The great composer and musical philosopher John Cage said, "If you want to listen to some music, open your window and listen." This is very, very true. When I'm driving down a street, I hear rhythms in all the objects that go past my vision. Especially telephone poles. I love telephone poles. I've sped up or slowed down the car just to keep a groove going!

Most importantly, we drummers should think about music in a non-drumming way. This will make us *all* better musicians!

•

The **Mental** Ward

Besides having the ability to play your instrument, the psychological aspects of recording play a big part in session work. Here's a little story from my past that hammers home this point.

In the summer of 1990 I was living in Los Angeles with my wife and our cat Bass (rhymes with "pass"). I was called to work on the upcoming Robbie Robertson album, *Storyville*. After pre-production, we were finally going into the studio.

The morning of my first day with Robbie, I carried my cymbals out to the car and saw Bass dead on the street in front of the house. I believe he was hit by a car and died early that morning. I loved this cat. He was a great guy. After crying my eyes out, I drove to the session.

The session started with Robbie's "Hold Back The Dawn," and all I could think of was Bassy and how he died before dawn. I told myself that I was going to play my heart out on this track for him. Well, we got started, but the producer stopped us after a couple of takes (twelve, actually…picky, picky, picky). He looked at me and said, "Billy, it's just about perfect, but your playing feels a bit too muscular. Try playing a bit more sensitively. Imagine that your favorite dog just died."

I couldn't believe he had said that. He had no idea about Bass and what had happened. I was speechless, totally embarrassed, and confused. I said, "I've gotta take a break. I'll be back in ten minutes."

I walked out of the session and all the way around the block (in LA—a *long* block). I was thinking about Bass and about playing for him. I was also thinking about how I was ruining this session (not to mention my career) with my preoccupation with him.

It was then that I realized how crucial it is in

Bass

art to be *detached*. To make the music work, I had to simply play the drums and be lost in the music—to be totally immersed in it. I shouldn't think about Bass, just as I shouldn't think *at all* when I'm playing. It was time to be a drummer. So I went back into the studio and simply played. *Afterwards*, I decided the track was for Bass. And it was.

There's an aspect of playing well that has to do with not caring too much. "Detach yourself from the world" is a phrase that is prevalent in almost all religions. It applies to music too.

•

Chapter 7

The **Practice** Of Drumming

Another Viewpoint

Practicing is an interesting concept. Tibetan monks practice meditation daily to quiet their minds. Doctors practice their medical skills. As for musicians, "He practiced on the bandstand" is a phrase and idea that is shunned. It means that the particular musician was overplaying, or at least not playing "in the moment."

Let's take a minute to think about our practice habits. Have you ever worked hard on your practicing, dedicated hours of concentrated work towards getting better at the drumset, and then on the gig experienced as much clumsiness as ever? I'm starting to wonder if when we practice working out of drum exercise books or on difficult licks, we're shutting our ears out of the musical act. When learning to do a difficult pattern, we're simply teaching our body to behave a certain way. Sometimes when I practice those kinds of

things, I feel like one of the Apollo chimps or a hamster in a cage. If I can just play that 32nd-note triplet with my feet, the light'll go off and I'll get fed—or get that gig I want.

Is it possible that when we work hard at our practicing, we're only becoming better *practicers* rather than better *players*? I've read that our human brain has two sides—a logical side and a creative side. I'm starting to think that practicing involves the side of our brain that is logical, the non-creative side. But when we're on a gig, we are *playing*—feeling the audience, feeling the other bandmembers, and feeling our own way as we play each song.

When things are right and I'm enjoying playing, I almost feel like I'm hovering in the air. I'm up there on kind of a creative tightrope. I think we should *practice* being on that creative tightrope so it isn't a strange,

Paul La Raia

"Is it possible that when we work hard at our practicing, we're only becoming better **practicers** rather than better players?"

unfamiliar feeling when it happens. For this, we need to be practicing *playing* instead of practicing practicing!

Why practice practicing? Well, duh...we all have to learn to drum if we're going to be drummers. But some folks like it so much, they're always figuring out new ways to do harder things on the drumset. Sure, it can be fun to see these technical-wonder musicians tear off unbelievable licks at music stores and clinics. It's even possible that there are bands somewhere that will let them display their amazing skills.

There's room in this world for everyone, so if you're really into technique, go for it. It's fine to work on technical things. Being able to execute our ideas is a part of our art. If a drum book or instructional video helps motivate and guide you to better technique, that's wonderful. When I was a teenager, I practiced endlessly on technical matters. I worked on things like stronger hands, and faster, more accurate rudiments. Also, reading skills and independence were important to me. These days, though, I accept the amount of technique that I have, so my practicing is focused on *playing*.

Sometimes I think drumming is like driving a car—it's that basic. When I was fifteen and learning to drive, driving a car seemed to be a fairly difficult thing. Now I don't have to think about it. Making music involves technique and vision, and when they match, it's art. If you can fully accept and embrace the amount of technique you already have, you can go for a drive!

In my book, Ringo Starr is a great example. When I listen to those Beatle records, I realize how musical pop drumming can be. It all becomes about *where you want to go*. To add just a bit more, I'll never forget a concert pianist telling me that Mozart was harder to play than Rachmaninoff because Mozart's music, in its simplicity, is more exposed!

How Do I Practice?

Let's say I have an hour to practice. The first fifteen minutes is spent on some technical matter, which, in my case, is maybe practicing how I can pick up that mallet in the middle of a song and not drop a beat while doing it. Or maybe it's getting a nice relaxed single-stroke roll going. I include tuning my drums in this portion of improvement, or vacuuming the teeny bits of wood on the carpet under the snare drum! After that, I spend the next forty-five minutes practicing *playing*.

First, I empty my brain of self-conscious thoughts and let my hands and feet start something. It's particularly interesting, but not necessary, if you limit the amount of "voices" that you're going to play with. I love starting with just the hi-hat, snare, and bass drum. Or, another favorite, playing just tom sounds with the snares turned off. That easily becomes very melodic and enchanting.

So I start playing. Since I'm not thinking, the odds are that it's in 4/4 time because I love 4/4 time and I don't have to think to play it. So, *it* has begun—I'm listening to what's unfolding from the drumset, almost witnessing the drumming. As a witness, I hear something (that accidentally happened) that sounds cool. So I step in with my brain and tell my hands and feet to repeat that groovy part I liked. I then repeat it successfully and move on...or, more likely, stumble at this point.

At some point there's always a stumble, probably because the sticking wasn't worked out.

(After all, I wasn't thinking!) So I go to that passage and figure it out. I've just learned a lick that my *ears* asked me to play. This is a lick that didn't come from a book or a mathematical equation. It came from my ears. Totally cool. I resume my playing as soon as possible.

Sometimes, over the course of a few weeks, I'll remember some of the new things that I've been learning and I'll repeat them in another practice/playing session. These things become my *vocabulary*, a part of my uniqueness. When I get up on the bandstand or I'm working in the studio, I'm less nervous because of my practice/playing moments. Even if I haven't had a gig in weeks, I've been playing!

I've found that in the last few years I've gotten a bit better at this kind of practicing. I even do it in my clinics—I'm now willing to risk a certain amount of embarrassment to demonstrate practicing in front of people. Practicing playing will, in my opinion, contribute to your musical self whether your technical level is a skateboard—or a race car! Give it a try. Let's become better players rather than better practicers.

•

Chapter 8

Passion And **Mechanics**

A General Rant About Drumming Habits

Sometimes I wonder what's going on inside a Formula One race-car driver's nervous system when he's tearing around the track at speeds of over two hundred miles an hour. Sheer, intense concentration for sure! One small mistake and... well...*splat*.

When ballet dancers "float" across the stage, the audience never sees how rock-solid the muscles that make that floating possible really are. They also don't see the equally solid concentration. A dancer once told me that the emotion of a dance happens only for the audience. If a dancer tries to emote while dancing, the dance is ruined. The dancer is living inside his or her mechanics.

What about drumming? I learned a long time ago that for me to emulate Keith Moon's wild and abandoned sound, I actually had to be relatively calm inside. When you're playing the "triumphant" encore at Bill & Ted's

Excellent Concert Theme Park (the biggest gig for your band all year), are your emotions "contained within your art"—or are you hyperventilating? This is one of those issues that we all want to figure out. And I suspect the answer is different and personal for each of us.

If you're playing mostly live gigs, a studio session is an unusual event. So it automatically raises your excitement and intensity. It did for me when I first started getting studio work. Wow...I'm making a tape.... I'm making a record.... Better have a few extra cups of coffee, 'cause I gotta stay sharp!

I'd bet that drummers who do their work almost exclusively in studios get equally worked up when that rare live gig approaches. When I got the call to tour with Joan Osborne, I was thrilled with the idea of getting to see people dance and scream to what I was playing. (True, some producers dance and scream

"It's important to understand that being 'in the moment' doesn't necessarily mean playing something **different** each time."

behind the console in the studio. But it's not too attractive.)

Developing Habits

Let's assume we play mostly rehearsals and live gigs, as opposed to studio recording sessions. Whether we're practicing songs with a band or practicing exercises alone in our rehearsal room, we are repeating some things that will eventually become habits. Naturally these include physical actions that will be "remembered" by our body. But I believe that how we use our hands or how we move our toes on the pedals is just the tip of the habit iceberg.

While physical habits of drumming are an obvious area of discussion, what about the habit of listening...or responding in the moment and truly playing *with* your bandmates? Do you ever play in an emotionally empty way? By that I mean playing the parts, but not being really involved with the music. Just "phoning it in," so to speak. The single most important habit I always focus on is to not be "asleep at the wheel" when I'm playing.

It's important to understand that being "in the moment" doesn't necessarily mean playing something different each time. There are situations in which I totally know what the

right groove for a song is, and even what the fills will be. I've messed around enough in soundchecks or rehearsals to know that there are no better notes in the world than those particular notes. The song just *loves* those notes, and I'm sure as heck not going to change them. However, when I'm performing the song, it's my job to make those notes sound and feel as if I'd just thought of them that very moment! Even though I know everything I'm going to play ahead of time, I try to place it in present tense.

Once in a while, of course, you have to break your own rules. A personal example of my *not* being inside the music took place five or six years ago. I was playing a film session with some seriously difficult odd-meter music. There I was, playing and trying to maintain "order." But it was just too darned hard (I like playing in four!) and everything was starting to fall apart. So for the sake of successfully completing the session, I started counting while I was playing. I had to. My ears simply weren't going to pull me through this one. This was a break in my habit-rule about always being in the moment and playing in the present tense. But had I not done so, I wouldn't have been able to get through

"Opinions and perspective are two prerequisites for **creating** art."

the composition without completely falling apart. I knew that if that happened, the producers might never call me again for sessions that I'm actually pretty good at. (The good news is, I knew what to practice for a while after that session!)

Establishing An Aesthetic

Being in the moment reaches beyond playing. I extend this maintain-the-intensity attitude to my listening habits, too. Because of my commitment to paying attention and loving every musical moment, there are many types of music that I honestly can't stand. They say there's no love if there's no hate, and my hate extends to things like "easy jazz." (That's a term that strikes me as self-contradictory, like "military intelligence.") There are other styles of music that I hate as well, but I'll keep them private for the time being.

Now, before I get tons of angry letters, let me say that I'm not *at all* knocking people who play or listen to these types of music. I've just personally made my aesthetic different from that kind of stuff. I do this to obey my personal law of music, which is: Be there...*always*. I make "being there" as detailed as possible. Opinions and perspective are two prerequisites for creating art.

Walking The Tightrope

Where am I going with this rant? I guess I'm saying that the art of music is a tightrope between physicality and spirituality, and between emotions and rational thought. This isn't a new concept, but I think it bears reconsidering. As we learn to play our instruments, we hopefully learn about ourselves, too. As we play or compose music, we express our uniqueness. As we begin to gain an aesthetic of our own, we learn habits that help us to express that aesthetic. Put enough of this together and we become good drummers, good musicians, and good people.

As an exercise, try thinking about various personal attributes and how they can apply to music. For example: honesty. What musician can you think of who is honest? I heard a lot of honest performances at the 2001 *Modern Drummer* Festival. Restraint... joyfulness...even compassion can be musical attributes.

Consider the habits you might have as a person and a musician. See if they fit your aesthetic. Maintaining art inside an emotional situation is a hard thing to do. There's a very real world out there, as well as inside each of us. In order to be unique musicians, we need to travel through that world and pay attention to it—and then to learn about ourselves through the experience. We need to recognize our individual habits, and think about how we can better utilize them as the tools of our drumming craft.

•

Chapter 9

The Mechanics Of **Excellent** Driving

Mechanisms Of Time

"Keeping time." What a strange phrase. I'm a drummer, but I don't keep time. I don't own it. I *observe* time. At best, when I play, I slice through time like a knife through pie, marking it at musical intervals. This process makes me feel like a very intricate Swiss watch full of tiny gears and levers. The wheels and levers inside my head constantly spin and measure, keeping me informed and helping me to gauge my pace.

We've all played gigs where the leader has *no* time, and we're drumming away feeling like we're trying to keep the Titanic from sinking. We get all the blame, and the "time phobia" begins.

These days, some producers judge our drumming by looking at it on a computer screen, instead of listening to the track. But let's not freak out about it. In today's recording environment there are some drummers who can bury a click by playing in perfect time. Other drummers may play a teeny bit around the click, giving the music

a more personal character. I tend to favor "character" players over "perfect" players, but both types of drummers have a place in a pro environment. It's all music, and each person's music reflects his humanity.

I hope you have an opinion on this. Whether you agree or disagree, developing your aesthetic is important to your musical growth. The previous chapter spoke mostly about habits and emotion. It promised some hard-core information. I'm going to share some seriously personal things in this essay; I hope they help you to better find your way on your musical path.

Getting Started

I'm going to begin with the assumption that your drumset is arranged so that you don't have to reach too far to hit any particular object. If that *isn't* the case, change it! Make your drumset your ally. I speak of this in depth at my clinics, because I believe that an inefficient drumk-

41

"Baseball pitchers all speak about their **mechanics**. Pitching a baseball over ninety miles an hour is much more physical than drumming. I think we can learn from these guys."

it setup is the prime reason that many drummers have bad time. Also, if you're not sure about how best to hold your sticks, take a lesson with someone who's "been there and done that." If you feel that no one in your area can help you, the legendary Jim Chapin is at many drummer functions, like the *Modern Drummer* Festival. Jim is a great (and in my opinion, accurate) source of information about grip. I'm grateful that he shares his knowledge with us all. That said, here we go.

Creating The Mechanism

I sometimes scare people when I say that we should get more mechanical in our drumming. That's because people think I mean to *play* mechanically, without feeling. That's definitely *not* what I mean. I mean we should operate like a watch. *Become the mechanism* of good time and tempo. And employ your own mechanisms to help you do that.

Let's say you're on a really big gig and you're just too darned excited. You're not operating according to your normal habits. Well, those

habits that you normally have can become tools that I call mechanisms. How high you raise your backbeat hand...the feeling of the stick in your hand...the feeling in your hand when you play the ride cymbal...the height of your seat...your posture...even the volume at which you're playing, and the sound of your drums...all these habits can come to your aid in a time of distress. You're hyperventilating? Thinking too much to really play inside the music? Feeling extra clumsy? Consult your habits! Make them mechanisms to propel you into the right artistic "zone."

Baseball pitchers all speak about their mechanics. Pitching a baseball over ninety miles an hour is much more physical than drumming. I think we can learn from these guys. When Hall of Fame pitcher Tom Seaver played baseball, he'd speak about his pitching "mechanics," and how maybe he failed that day because he didn't "stay inside himself." After hearing other baseball pitchers speak, I realized that "staying inside myself" means obeying my mechanics and allowing my body to become a mechanism. So I'm not talking

Paul La Raia

about becoming mechanical. I'm talking about having mechanisms that are based on good habits. Seek good mechanisms and employ them every time you play. Allow your whole self to become a mechanism.

Habit/Mechanism Idea #1: Outward Emotion

Get into the habit of maintaining the same emotional zone when you play the drums, no matter the gig or obstacle. Big gig? Lame gig? Not your drumset? Get over it! Take note of your emotional state when you play a good, solid gig, and try to live there every moment of every day. Whether it's a live gig in front of eighty thousand people or for one person, a studio session or a jam session—make it all the same, as far as your approach is concerned. Get mechanical (in a good way) about this.

Habit/Mechanism Idea #2: The Physical World

Observe all your physical habits as often as possible. This topic could be a book unto itself, but

here are a few ideas.

How do you play your snare drum? How high do you raise your sticks? What's up with your wrist angle and your grip? Take mental snapshots of all these things and more: your hands...your feet...your posture...your throne height...your pedal tension. Listen to what your muscles tell you. Are you relaxed?

I've found that employing this mechanism (along with #1 above) can get me into a playing zone under all kinds of awful conditions. But there are still times, even when I have both mechanisms happening, that I'm still totally unattached to the music—and starting to panic! Which leads me to...

Habit/Mechanism Idea #3: Breathing

Feeling distracted? Starting to panic? Remembering the mechanism of how I breathe can get me back to playing the music. Mechanisms #1 and #2 can help here too. (They *all* help each other.) But it's important to remember that there are other things to look for beyond the feeling of the stick on the drumheads—non-drumistic things.

I try to be aware of the sounds inside my body as the "wheels turn." There *is* something down there in my stomach when I'm playing. What is it? Hamsters in a cage? A ferris wheel? Whatever it is, it will show up and help me out once I get enough mechanism "wheels" turning. Drummers with good time usually know when they have sped up or slowed down because something in their stomach told them as it happened.

A Simple Exercise

Cool so far? I hope so. There are many other mechanisms. Different tempos require different mechanisms. When I play really slowly, I add more "wheels" inside my body so I can flow through the time without playing more notes. What do I mean? Oceans have an undertow. So do rhythms!

Let's take a 4/4 pattern at a slow tempo, say 45 bpm (beats per minute). If you don't have a metronome, just focus on playing really slow. Now, play quarter notes with your ride hand. Were you sub-dividing between the quarter notes inside your head? Were they 8th notes? 16th notes? Try triplets inside your head as you play the quarter notes. How about quarter-note triplets? And if you really want to up the ante, try half-note triplets.

Time Out

Have you discovered any mechanisms as you've been practicing? Go back to the simple stuff above and *feel* the stick in the hand. Does it feel like it always does? Is your posture the same as usual?

Now play an entire beat with all your limbs on the drumset, at any tempo that is comfy for you. Check your mechanisms as you play. Can you find new mechanisms just for you?

Back To The Example

Let's go back to the terribly slow quarter notes. Only now, add the other limbs and play the most simple, exposed beat you can at 45 bpm.

It's *hard* to play this slow. At least it is if you truly care about tempo and musicality. There isn't enough movement with our bodies at this slow tempo to fill the space with mechanisms. So when this happens, I utilize parts of my body that don't make a sound. For example, my mouth. Try singing a melody while you're playing. Now you're accompanying a soloist with your quarter notes. It's far more musical than 8th notes!

When I play slow tempos, I make noises. Microphones don't seem to mind the sounds that I make, and it helps me to groove inside the rhythm. The late Jeff Porcaro did the same thing. In fact, many drummers do it. John Riley once told me that jazz great Elvin Jones started making noises as a young drummer. It seems his teacher suggested making a vocal sound when there were rests in the music, as a way for Elvin to follow the rests and not play through them. That teacher was smart. He gave Elvin a mechanism.

I'll also use both of my heels to help mark time. You can do this no matter what your pedal technique happens to be. Whichever heel isn't playing at the moment is available for a little movement. Just a small click on the heel plate can help keep you inside the groove.

What sort of mechanisms you utilize is not really important. What is important is that you have them available to call on, in order to help you feel comfortable and confident within yourself, no matter what the musical situation. When all that is going on, then the *total* mechanism that is you, the drummer, will be running like that proverbial Swiss watch: smoothly, efficiently, and accurately.

•

Chapter 10

Good-Time Sessions

Play Well And Have Fun In The Studio

In this article we're going to get into the realities of studio recording. We'll focus on methods you can employ to help you play with good time—and *have* a good time—in session situations.

Of course, all recording sessions are different. But for the sake of this article I'm going to talk about doing a popular music session where a lot of overdubbing will be done after the so-called "basic" drum track is recorded. This is a more common practice than having everyone "pouring cement" together, live, in the studio.

A Bring-Along List

As a starting point, here's a quick list of extra things to bring to a session:

An extra snare drum. It's amazing how changing a snare drum can make the whole drumset sound different.

Extra cymbals. You never know which of your cymbals might be more "mic'-friendly."

Headphones. Bring the headphones that you're used to and comfortable with. Some demo-type studios don't have closed-cup headphones, because they cost more. But we drummers prefer closed-cup headphones, so if you have a set, bring it!

Headphone amp or mixer. A weak power amp can be helped with a small Mackie-type mixer, or by a smaller headphone amp. Peavey makes a reliable and inexpensive headphone amp. Also bring all necessary cables. Don't count on the studio to have the cables you need.

Percussion. I always bring some percussion toys, shaker sticks, Rods and other alternative sticks, brushes...all that kind of stuff. Even on basic tracks the percussion or shaker sticks might be needed to make the track feel better or enable you to play the basic track better.

Water, towel, and an extra shirt—for obvious reasons. Maybe deodorant for later, too!

It's All In The Mix

When it comes to playing successfully in a studio, one of the most important things to know about is the mix. I don't mean the sound of the drums in the control room. I'm talking about what we drummers have in our headphone mix. Knowing what kind of mix we need during a session is an important aspect of successful recording. I suspect these choices are different for each person.

I'm going to assume (hope) that you are not cursed with a studio that has no flexibility in its headphone cue mix. Unfortunately, many "starter" studios have a very bad headphone cue system, because they've put their investment into their microphones and mixing board. This is too bad, because when musicians can't hear, they can't play very well, no matter what. If you're shopping for a studio to record your band's demo in, check the headphone cue system. Does it have enough power? Are there enough separate cue "sends" available?

The mix, or volume, of different instruments *totally* affects a groove. Listen to your favorite grooves from records. Check out the other non-percussion instruments in terms of what *they* are doing for the drummer's groove. In James Brown's music, *everybody's* a drummer. The guitar players are conga players! It's important for you to train your ears to notice these kinds of things.

Great producers know how the right timing from a guitar—or even from a singer—can make or break a groove. If these separate items are mixed wrong, the groove is also killed. That's why people who mix records are so important to

their success that they get their own credit (not to mention payment). Obviously, if the mix is important for the song, it's also important for us drummers in order for us to give a great performance.

Tricks Of The Trade

Here are some rules that work for me, and that you might try next time you're wearing a set of headphones in a studio. We'll start with a quote from Bruce Gaitsch, one of the best rhythm guitar players I've ever played with: "Want to groove more? Listen to everybody but yourself!"

When I'm in the studio, half the time I have the drums out of my headphone mix entirely. If I have myself in the mix, it's just a feather of me— just enough to let me be in the same room as everyone else. After all, I'm playing the drums, I've tuned them, and I know how they sound. For several years I've been using headphones that cut out 24 dB or so, and I'm used to them. I know that the drums will sound good if my physical and emotional habits (my mechanics) are in place. So I don't concern myself with how I sound. Instead, I try to swim inside the song.

Who gets into my mix? Anyone who will help me play a great take. Listen to what everyone is playing, and figure out if they're aiding you. Sometimes the guitarist is playing a pattern in each chorus that really helps me sit inside the groove. So he gets to stay in my mix. In fact, that guitar will be a mechanism to help me groove during the choruses!

In popular music, the vocal is crucial to my playing. It will be the loudest item in the mix at the end, so I have to hear it—and understand the words. The drum track has to complement the vocal. On the other hand, if the singer's time isn't incredible, I learn the song as soon as possible (during run-through) and then have the vocals turned way down. This way I *feel* the

Paul La Raia

"If they don't get a great drum track—meaning a great performance from you—then the record is going **nowhere**!"

vocal, but the attacks of the consonants won't disrupt my flow.

When you're working at a studio where the engineer controls your mix, ask the engineer (quietly and confidentially) to remove some of the bandmates that are not helping you. Just walk into the booth and ask if the talkback mic' is off. (Always be aware of the many mic's around you that might possibly be on.) Then have the engineer remove the offenders from your mix. He or she will do this because *you, as the drummer, are all that counts right now* to everybody in the recording process. If they don't get a great drum track—meaning a great performance from you—then the record is going nowhere!

By the way, it's also permissible to ask a guitar player or keyboardist to change a phrase so you can play your track better. He's going to replace his track later anyway, right? So make him your ally. In fact, get the whole band on your side! Remember my previous articles about mechanisms? The parts that your band plays can be mechanisms for your drumming, just as much as your physical body can.

I should mention the "dark side" before we leave this section. What if *everybody* stinks?

What if there are *no* allies to have in the mix? It happens. Under those circumstances, the click certainly becomes more important! I'll add to the click by playing a tambourine part that "signals" the choruses and bridge.

What about out-of-time bandmates? See if the engineer can compress their parts with a fast attack to lesson the volume of their downbeats. Or try taking the treble off their sounds to ease their attack. If their volume is right (just barely loud enough for you to hear), you'll be able to play while you sort of "imagine" that they are all there with you.

Click track volume? I like the click to be loud enough that it's kind of like a neighbor next door just hammering away while I'm playing. I *hear* it, but I'm not really *listening* to it. Maybe a better way to put it is this: While drumming, we're driving the car. (Obviously I like this car-analogy stuff.) When we're heading down the perfectly in-time highway, there are telephone poles flying past, just outside our field of vision. Those telephone poles are the click track. The click is an impartial witness to (and participant in) the music. It's just there, like oxygen in the air. If I have to strain to hear the click in my headphone mix, then it isn't loud enough, or my mix is wrong. If I'm listening for the click, then I'm not in the moment of playing. Doh! I've become a carpenter, not a musician.

What The Pros Say

I recently sent out a questionnaire on this elusive subject of keeping time to some pro drummer friends. Here are a few relevant answers about click tracks:

Q. Do you prefer a regular click, or some other timekeeper?

A. From Pat Mastelotto (King Crimson): "It depends on the feel of the song. For most shuffles, fast tempos, or if I'm tracking with a rhythm section and sharing one cue mix, I use a quarter- or 8th-note click. But most often I write a pattern in a beatbox. Usually my pattern is busy: shaker 16ths, hi-hat 8ths, sidestick or cowbell quarter notes, and a percolating rhythm on congas or ethnic drums."

The following additional statement shows Pat's maturity as a musician: "It's also important to know what the end result will be. If I know they're not keeping any machine tracks, I can bend time. My fills can rush. But if they plan to keep elements from a sequencer, loop, or beatbox, I have to play much tighter to the click—since my bending might make others seasick later."

Q. If you prefer a pattern, or a pattern added to the click, do you prefer a programmed drum machine pattern? A loop? Or do you play something on the spot in the studio to drum along to later?

A. From Pat Mastelotto again: "I do all three, depending on the artist/vibe/studio time/feel of the track. I like to do this in pre-production (rehearsal) so I can try out ideas before the studio clock is ticking."

A. From Paul DeLong (independent Toronto session drummer and clinician): "I usually leave the quarter-note click intact and add a shaker playing the 16ths, 8ths, triplets, or whatever subdivision is needed. I might also put an upbeat accent on the shaker pattern to get a nice up-down thing going on. Then I might add handclaps or tambourine on 2 and 4 to give it more feel."

A. From Randy Cooke (also independent Toronto session drummer and clinician): "I prefer to have a simple, tight shaker or hi-hat giving me the 8th-note feel, and a side stick for the quarter notes. In all cases, I like the 8th-note feel to be a little louder. After all, when playing most pop music, the second you're locked with the click, the quarter-note feel disappears. As for loops, the only time I dig playing with them is if they're actually going to be used in the track."

Randy's point about adding 8ths because "the second you're locked with the click, the quarter feel disappears" is great. Solving the challenge of playing with great timing involves creating parts that are reliable contrasts—well-timed "backdrops" in the mix. This can be accomplished by having other musicians with great time in your mix, or by adding other aids like those mentioned above.

Use Every Mechanism

So what's the bottom line? To play in time—whether with a click or without—we drummers need as many specific mechanisms as we can muster. Some we create from within ourselves, some we get from our training. And some, like those outlined in this article, are outside aids that we can employ to make our work easier and our performances better.

•

Chapter 11

Undertow

A Good Mechanism For Your Time

I'd like to share some thoughts on "undertow," the contrasting rhythms that can help us play better. This is the stuff that nobody talks about. Most drummers probably don't even *think* about it. But we should. Here are some exercises designed to tune and polish our "inner gears."

Let's start with what most would say is the simplest rock beat.

Play this sucker at a medium tempo. (If you have a metronome, set it at quarter note = 120 for a reference tempo.) This could be a drum track for Steely Dan's "Hey Nineteen," The Doobie Brothers' "Takin' It To The Streets," or (you fill in the blank). It's one of the easiest beats, and it's one of the most common in popular music. But it's also a cool beat!

How can we make this beat feel great? With undertow. To get started, while playing this beat, set your "inner gears" at 8th notes. This is the easy, "default setting" for most drummers' inner clocks because it follows the fast limb—in this case, your dominant hand playing the hi-hat.

Now play the same beat, but inside feel a 16th-note undertow. Don't *play* the 16ths, just feel 'em. It's the exact same beat, we're simply changing the undertow we're feeling inside. You'll notice subtle things start to happen to the groove when you do this. For me, the hi-hat accents automatically change. It almost feels more like a U2 track—or something heavier, like some grunge feels.

Let's try this same concept with a shuffle rhythm. Start with the following simple shuffle.

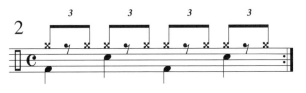

This beat reminds me of John Lennon's "Instant Karma." Now go back to it, but inside feel an 8th-note-triplet undertow. Check out how naturally important each downbeat becomes with that triplet undertow.

Apparently some younger drummers have trouble feeling triplet undertow. What's up with all of you guys who aren't as comfy with triplets as you are with duple rhythms? It seems that the least comfortable undertow (and groove) is triplet-based. Admittedly, there are a lot fewer songs these days with shuffle or swing feels. But, believe me, triplets are cool.

Triplet-based grooves are much more fun than duple rhythms like 8ths and 16ths. Yes, they're a bit harder. Sticking, for one thing, gets confusing. And when you build more rhythms on top of triplets, it quickly becomes more complicated. But let's take a look at this. Can you play "3 over 2"?

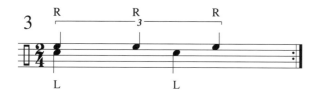

There are many different ways to learn to play 3 over 2. The obvious way is to slow it down, start with one hand, and then have that hand continue on "auto-pilot" while you add the second hand. Another way to look at it, though, is to see it from a "birds-eye view," as if it's one thing.

Classical drummers will, when sightreading, frequently lead with their strong (let's say right) hands. (Lefties, just reverse what I'm saying here; I know, you're used to it!) So read the following pattern and play it leading with your right hand on all downbeats.

Now add the left on each downbeat as well, in unison with your right hand.

Now move your left hand to a different ashtray or whatever you're near so it has a different sound from your right. You're now playing 3 against 2. Try reversing this pattern and making it 2 against 3. How about alternating the sticking?

Can you play this on your leg? Can you *sing* it? If so, go back to example 1 (the even 8th-note pattern) and add a triplet undertow inside the 8th-note pattern. If you're doing this, notice how the downbeats feel differently and how you feel more confident on each quarter note. Why? Because there are more details happening before each quarter note passes.

When I'm in trouble with my time in the studio or on a bandstand, I'll try a more complex undertow to help lock me into the groove. I feel a greater "lock" with the tempo doing this. I have absolutely no idea if other drummers do this, but this works for me. If

"Inside our guts are wheels and gears that could be helping us with our timing—or they can lie dormant. I say get out the **WD-40**, grease 'em up, and turn 'em loose!"

your singer bumps into your ride cymbal, and the guitar player rushes like crazy, if you use undertow you're *still* going to be able to "hold down the fort."

Please spend some time playing grooves and not concerning yourself with more notes, faster tempos, and better fills. Instead play a beat and keep playing it. Go inside yourself and see what's going on. What's your undertow? Can you change it freely to other types of subdivisions in time? Can you have a multiple, complex undertow going while you're playing? Inside our guts are wheels and gears that could be helping us with our timing—or they can lie dormant. I say get out the WD-40, grease 'em up, and turn 'em loose!

I think it's crucial for all of us drummers to be able to comfortably swim in not only 8th-note and 16th-note undertows, but all kinds of triplet undertows. Even when I'm playing a simple 8th-note groove, I've got some triplet wheels turning inside as well. I'm truly comfy with tapping and feeling "3 over 2," "3 over 4," and even "5 over 3."

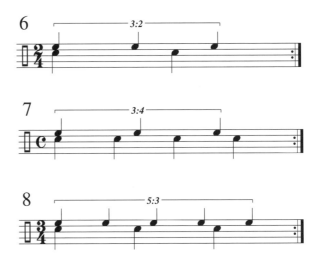

These more odd subdivisions will probably only show themselves in things like little press rolls that I might play on the snare as a small detail to the large groove, but it's in there somewhere. If I'm not playing it with my hands, it's at least inside my stomach as part of my undertow.

There's more to this. The undertow is easier to find (and less important to solely rely upon) when the tempo happens to be near the pace of our heartbeat. But when the tempo is either extremely slow or fast, we really need the undertow and all those little gears inside.

Think about it: When you're playing a really

slow beat, don't you add more subdivisions until the groove is ticking away near your heartbeat? Go back to example 1 and play it at an incredibly slow tempo. Get it to groove with confidence. I'd bet the farm that you're feeling 16ths under this tempo.

Let's say the chorus goes to a quarter-note feel on the bell of the ride. If you're accomplished at playing, singing, and feeling 3 over 2, add a triplet undertow inside while playing those quarter notes on the bell. This should make you feel *really* locked into the tempo and groove. Interesting stuff, huh?

How about playing quick tempos? Play example 1 at some ridiculously fast tempo. Getting tired? Hard to keep up with confidence? Undertow can help with this too. Let's learn how to apply undertow to this by first making the pattern a half-time groove.

Now it's somehow a bit easier to play, because we're feeling our undertow more

slowly. Here's the cool part: Go back to example 1 at the same, ridiculously fast tempo, but feel it in half-time. It's easier to play. Now how about feeling it in *double* half-time, twice as slow? Some jazz musicians I know call this feeling in "big time." This is how they feel those extremely fast tempos. They're only feeling each downbeat as the measures go racing by. Get it? Maybe if we remember this concept of big time, we'll play those fast tempos better.

I realize I've fished around a bit in trying to explain some of these time concepts, but I'm hoping this leads to some thought and study on your part. Maybe you'll eventually experience an improvement in your playing with your band or with a click track. (I hate seeing so many drummers intimidated by click tracks!) Click tracks, rhythmic undertows, and other mechanisms can enable us to play with more confidence and accuracy. But even more importantly, they'll give us piece of mind.

Chapter 12

Fantasy And **Truthfulness**

A Hard Look At The Business...And Yourself

Want to be a star? Limos, chicks, great monitors, free drums, lots of money, mints on the pillow, laundry service, free Nikes? Do you still believe in this dream? "I'll practice. I'll get good enough. I'll work on my hair and my waistline, and then I'll get in a band and reap all the rewards!" Oh, if it was only this way.

Sorry, It's A Fantasy

I hate to say it, but the music business is a nasty place. Some of the people that control the flow of the business are not particularly kind. They'll cheat you or take advantage of you if it suits them. One of the reasons that they can get away with these shenanigans is that there are too many of us willing to kill our mothers just to fulfill the dream of being on that big stage. Share a room with four others? No problem. The gig only pays so much? Great. Rock on!

I feel you have to look beyond these dreams of stardom and come up with a healthy goal. In fact, my goal remains to play in the moment and to be completely sympathetic to the music. That may not sound like much, but actually, it's a lot. If you're dreaming of earthly rewards, it's likely that you'll be bitterly disappointed. On the other hand, loving art and striving to be a wonderful artist can lead to a very complex and fulfilling life.

My self-respect has nothing to do with who I'm working with or how impressive my résumé is. All that matters to me is how I'm playing *today*. The rest of it—the press, the lights, the bad monitors (I wonder if U2 has to deal with bad monitors?), the fans, the free Diet Coke—doesn't matter. I'm over it already.

If you're fifteen years old and have only played at a school dance, you probably have a nightmarish story about the music business. Here's one of mine. I once worked with an

Paul La Raia

"My self-respect has nothing to do with who I'm playing with or how **impressive** my résumé is. All that matters to me is how I'm playing today."

artist who called me a week before we were to leave on a tour of China to tell me he was going to do the tour with a different drummer. (Actually, he had a manager call me at 2:30 in the morning to leave a message on my service.) And I thought this artist was one of my friends! I had even planned my family's vacation around the trip. I thought that this guy was a mammal, a warm-blooded, creative, and sensitive person. Well, I found out otherwise.

How about that band you're in and that recording you're planning? You've all saved money, booked the studio time, and hired "Mr. Snazzy Guy," a producer who has worked with a few name artists. He says he's going to make you sound great. But once the recording begins, everyone in your band except you gets psycho and does so many drugs that they couldn't tell a great take if it bit them on the butt! And you're stuck there, wondering what's up with all the new tempos. You're spending your downtime in this expensive studio planning on quitting the band and wondering how it all went wrong.

I apologize if this article seems too negative, but sometimes bad things happen in life, and we have to try to overcome them without receiving lasting scars. And that's tough to do.

Truthfulness

The other side of the equation in working (and surviving) in this business is truthfulness. In fact, it's an important tool for getting better. Accept no deceit! That means no deceit in business affairs, but more importantly in personal affairs *and* in musical affairs. You especially don't want to lie to yourself about your playing. Listen to yourself harshly. The notes have to be right. Make the music special.

Here are a couple of questions you might want to ask yourself about your playing. Remember, be honest.

Q) Is it hard to control yourself in the studio? Can you resist the urge to play all of your "cool" ideas?

A) What I've found is, in time, when you listen to sessions you've done, the sessions that you played more of your "great new ideas" on will be the ones that you can't stand. The sessions on which you simply "played the music" will be good.

Bonus tip: I speak a lot about incorporating

alternative sounds (shaker mallets, rods, etc.) into drumming. But if you aren't comfortable with these types of tools, you should stay away from using them in a pressure studio or gig situation. It's your bottom-line musical habits that stand out. You can't stop them or control them. They are exposed, audible to all, and obvious—just like the color of your eyes.

Q) Can I play to a click and make it feel great? How exactly "on" the click do I have to be?

A) The better, real-record-making producers don't watch a screen to check your timing. They do, however, have a very highly developed sense of beat and time. Beats and timing are a large part of what hit records are all about. You don't have to be dead on the click (don't stop trying, of course), but you do need to play exactly the same way with the click from measure to measure for a track to be considered a keeper.

For example, if you're consistently behind a bit with your backbeats and it feels good, that's fine. But if one measure is behind and another measure is some other way... well...chances are good a worthy producer

will feel it and want a better take (or a better drummer).

That said, please keep in mind that it takes a rhythm section to make a groove, even though all fingers get pointed at us drummers when things aren't feeling right. I'm convinced that part of being a great drummer is the ability to recognize what's wrong with a group's feel and to be able to correct it, maybe by drumming differently, by changing the headphone cue mix, or by making a verbal suggestion to one of the other players.

A Happy Ending?

Some folks are more interested in "making it" than in playing well. If that's your goal, music will be an awful business. Believe me, it takes a great love of music to survive. Honestly, do you put *all* of your effort into playing great? If your answer is yes, then you have a chance—and only a chance. That's the ante in the poker game that is this business.

Be well—and *play* well.

Chapter 13

A **Change** Is Gonna Come

Staying Open To New Music

I was recently listening to some bluegrass music, which I've fallen head over heels in love with due to the soundtrack of *Oh Brother, Where Art Thou?* This music has no drums on it whatsoever, but I *love* it. I particularly love the simplicity of the songs, the pure passion of the vocalists, and the sound of the beautiful acoustic instruments. (The guitarists all have great time, by the way.)

I played this stuff for a friend, who is a wonderful writer, producer, and player of another style of music. But then he started talking over it almost immediately. An hour later, he asked if I was getting into "country music" lately. But the thought occurred to me, Can we only dig what *we* do? Or does our openness to new music end at a certain age or experience? As we get older, do our ears get as brittle as our joints and bones do? Is there such a thing as aural osteoporosis?

Maybe this attitude should be called "narcis-sistic listening," meaning we'll only listen to music that directly has to do with *us*. Does the music have to be our style for us to relate to it? Why is that? Maybe we aren't as good as what we're listening to and it makes us feel bad.

Now I'm going to get blunt. I'd bet there are some drummers who don't appreciate more simplistic music, because they don't have the chops. What kind of chops do I mean? I mean having the ears to see the grace, charm, and love of a simple piece of music—just as much as the ability to hear and be thrilled by complex harmonies and technically complex music. How do we keep an open mind to new ideas in art when it's so darned comfortable to stick with what we already know? Can we relate to things outside our sphere?

I believe the answer is yes, but we have to sometimes grow in baby steps. If you have a desire to better understand jazz, don't start with John Coltrane and Elvin Jones. Try a George

"How do we keep an open mind to new ideas in art when it's so darned comfortable to stick with what we **already** know?"

Shearing album, or albums by other artists such as Wes Montgomery, early George Benson, Jimmy Smith, or Art Blakey. You want to get more into rock? Use the same principles. Ease into it.

There's never any shame in asking what to listen to. I'm always asking my friends, What are you listening to? When they give an enthusiastic answer about something I haven't heard, I pick it up right away. Those are the best times—finding something *new*.

Developing New Habits

It takes patience to get into new stuff. When I hear a different-sounding song, unfamiliar chords, or an odd-sounding singer, I have to apply some patience to listen to it. Some styles of music have a technique that doesn't have to do with ripping off double paradiddles at 250 bpm. (Ask the guitar player in your band to play a picking part of even 16ths on his guitar, say at 110 bpm, and go through some simple rhythm changes. See how he does.) Playing something at a moderate tempo, but playing it even and with control, can be very hard to do. It took me a long time just to be able to play even 16ths on the darned hi-hat!

Some things are harder than they sound, and some things are easier than they sound. Do you think there exists a kind of mental technique or

aesthetic chops? I do. I think there are people who have many *physical* drumming skills, but don't have the kind of chops to listen and enjoy seemingly less complex music.

Earlier I mentioned the idea of not being as good as what we are listening to, and having that feeling affect our taste. But sometimes we catch the disease of being "above" a type of music as well. Folk music could generally qualify as an example here. It's all about one's aesthetic or perspective.

If this were a folk magazine, we might be talking about being "above" Buddy Rich: "Oh, that Buddy Rich is just too aggressive...too much testosterone...I'm interested in more subtle shades." Please don't misunderstand. I'm not saying that music by Buddy Rich, or Metallica for that matter, isn't good stuff. We're drummers, so the faster, rowdier stuff has an obvious appeal to us all.

I believe in a perfect world where people can love the harmony and beauty of a Chet Baker ballad, or bagpipe music, and then turn around and put on a David Bowie, Jeff Beck, or Buddy Rich CD. (I'm sticking with Bs here just for fun.) Can't we learn things from all music, no matter our ability, taste, or influences? Isn't art above all these trivialities? I say "Out with musical snobbery!"

Chapter 14

Leap Of **Faith**

Having The Courage To Try Something New

Lately I've been thinking about Tom Everett Scott, the actor who learned to play the drums for the film *That Thing You Do*. I was hired as his tutor, and I spent quite some time with him privately and on the movie set. It's funny how things go in life. I used to wonder why I took that job. Well, hindsight is 20/20. Looking back, part of why I took the gig was because it was glamorous. It involved Tom Hanks, and it was very different from my other work, which was mostly uncredited, anonymous film scores and record sessions. But it turned out to be a pivotal experience for me.

Obviously, if you've seen the film, Tom E. Scott did a great job. But he was also a great student. He truly listened to everything I presented to him, responded honestly, and gave his best effort. He really *became* a drummer, and that blew my mind. You know, I wasn't teaching at the time I took that gig. I hadn't taught anything for twenty years. Now, besides working as a drummer, I'm teaching, writing for a drumming magazine, and doing drum clinics!

What brings such a change?

Many of us are looking for change with our

Fugino Sakai

> ## "For some reason, it's easier for some people to **jump** to a new place than for others. But each of us is capable of making the jump."

work—and wondering about our future. And this isn't exclusive to you twenty-year-olds. At times I think we *all* feel like we don't know what we're supposed to be doing, but we know that what we're doing isn't right. Maybe that gig or job is too boring or not challenging enough. It's at least not what we were put on this planet to do. But where do we go when this happens? My reminder is, again, just take what the universe gives to you. (You may be surprised.) Sometimes it's a little job accepted on impulse—or someone we've made friends with—that can dramatically change our lives.

Here are some qualities that we need if we want to move forward. First off, it takes courage to act on a new tangent. It isn't easy to travel across the country to have a drum lesson with someone you admire. Or to uproot your family and move to a (hopefully) more promising city that currently holds no promises for you. Or how about simply buying a CD that you're not sure you'll be able to listen to more than once (if that), but buying it anyway because maybe it'll teach you something *new*.

When I was a kid, I bought a Sun Ra album instead of a Jefferson Airplane album because I figured, based entirely on the cover design and the name of the artist, that I'd get something new out of this Sun Ra thingie. And I did.

Having a thirst, a great need for new experiences, can be a great motivation. Maybe impatience is a good quality after all. It's certainly not just courage for me. Sometimes I've done something out of desperation. I took that Tom-Hanks-tutor-the-actor gig out of desperation to avoid doing the same old thing yet again. Running away from something can be just as powerful as courage.

We could all use more growth, knowledge, and experience. If a jam situation or a gig exists that offers one of those things, I say take it. Jump on it. The water is not just fine— it's *new*. If there's nothing else out there at the time, choose movement. Being active and choosing movement over stagnancy will lead you to something new.

Mr. Ego

Nothing is ever totally black and white, of course. We can't act too rashly when we think an opportunity exists. We have to weigh stupidity against courageousness. I've got plenty of stupidity. And my stupidity car is mostly driven by Mr. Ego.

All artists have egos—I certainly do. It comes in handy sometimes. I believe that many artists also feel like frauds much of the time. After all, there's always so much that I could've played better. (Let's go to the "I suck" tape, reel three, take ten.) And there are always some situations that end up making us *feel* like a fraud. You know, that gig we did and never got paid, or the "you can't use this elevator, enter through the kitchen" bit, or you're finally getting to play with someone important to you and they seem to be in another world that day. (Was it me? Was I that bad?)

Anyone crazy enough to make art and believe in its importance in this world must have an ego just to carry on. My ego helps me believe that I'm not a total fraud. But there have been times in my life when it hurt me and kept me from truly listening and learning. We mustn't let our ego keep us away from something that might teach us.

Mirror, Mirror, On The Wall...

For a personal "reality check," look to your friends for a reflection of yourself. This is just like checking yourself on the tape recorder for a reflection of your playing. If you're great as a person or a musician, people will be telling you so. If you're not hearing that lately, then get back to work. If your ego says you're great but nobody else says so, then you need to get out of the house, out of the practice room, and into society—maybe even into some *therapy*.

In the end, taking off in a new direction requires faith. Faith is, to me, the belief in something unprovable, thus the phrase "leap of faith." It takes a leap of faith to go somewhere new. For some reason, it's easier for some people to jump to a new place than for others. But each of us is capable of making the jump.

Improving your gig really *is* all about dynamics, tone, touch, technique, experience, and getting better as a musician. It's also about getting better as a person, because the one doesn't happen without the other.

•

Chapter 15

Everybody Auditions

A Pro Offers A Few Tips

Maybe it's your band playing a twenty-minute set for free at a club's audition night. Or maybe it's an audition as a drummer—could be for a local band or a huge global tour. But no matter what the situation, *everybody* auditions.

I'm hopeful that some of my experiences and ideas will help you when you get the next big call. What follows is a list of things that I do to be prepared for an audition. If you follow these ideas, you'll gain a quiet confidence, because you'll be well prepared. At the very least, you'll become a better drummer. You never know, you may even get the gig!

Really and truly believe that you want the gig—or else you'll play badly. I don't prepare well unless I really want a gig. Let's say that for a certain band I'm auditioning for, during their tour I'll have to set a pig's head on my bass drum. I'll still try to convince myself that I truly

want that gig. Bring on the pig's head! (So obviously, a "Well, they won't offer it to me anyway" attitude is not allowed. No personal sabotage.)

Be yourself at the audition. When I first moved to New York, I found myself playing my first jingles. Back then, most of the other musicians on the jingle dates were mellow. They'd talk about their summer home, or kids—very pedestrian stuff. I tried to fit in by acting quiet and thoughtful. I figured I should keep a low profile. Then I realized that however I behaved wasn't going to change my amount of work. I realized that I should simply be myself and relax at these sessions. This was a major lesson for me. Behave as you normally do. Be *yourself*.

When the phone call comes, ask questions about the audition. "What songs will be played at the audition?" In pop music, there are usually two to six songs that they want to hear you play. Ask the question, and then go learn the stuff.

Also ask, "What can I bring to the audition?" A snare drum and bass pedal? An entire kit? Or nothing? Find out. Only ask the most important questions, and keep the discussion brief. The person who is talking to you may have to call ten or more other drummers who'll have the same questions, so be considerate. Humor, or at least a good nature, is always appreciated when discussing business on the phone.

So, only if time permits, ask when the tour is and how long it is. Money is always the tricky issue, isn't it? In my opinion, it's not appropriate to talk about money until after they want you. However, if you truly don't think they'll pay you enough even if they want you (and you don't want to do the audition without this information), bring up the money in a non-threatening way. For example, "What's the range of pay for other bands at this club?" Or if it's a touring gig, find out the ballpark salaries. Once I said, "I don't think I should audition. What if your artist wants me and you have to tell him that he can't afford me?" I ended up getting the gig, but to this day, I think it was rude of me to say that. But like I said, if it's a tour, don't talk dough until you've been asked to do the gig.

Know the audition songs as if you've been playing them for a year. My "quickie chart" really comes through for me here. (See Chapter 18 for a full explanation.) I haven't checked around much, but I'd venture to say that all pro drummers use some kind of system like mine to quickly learn and be able to remember songs. The process of writing everything down helps me to remember them. I first write out every important fill exactly as it appears on the record or audition tape, note for note. My quickie charts go through several "drafts" as I progress in learning the songs, so that by the time of the audition, it's a pretty darned small piece of paper.

Now we're into the debate of whether to play "your personal part" to the songs, or to play what you think they want. If there's a record of the song by the group you are auditioning for, learn that drum part *note for note*. Even if the band didn't like the drumming on the record at the time it was done (the take was kept because of the evil producer), that part is by now *very* familiar to the band and they're used to it. Furthermore, it's probably exactly what they're looking for from their next drummer as a gauge. So stick with the original vibe. Play the part as best you can and as close to the original feel as the recording or reference tape. That means details, details, details. Sure, the hi-hat is playing 8th notes, but what are the dynamics of the hat? Is it tough and even? Loud? What's the attitude? Kind of like Kenny Aronoff would play, or Mick Fleetwood, or Manu Katché? Dig in and study it closely and put it into your ears and hands.

Tape yourself playing to the audition material to make sure you sound perfect. As I've said before, you'll never lose your uniqueness no matter how much you submit to the old/original drum part. You'll shine through no matter what you do. On the other hand, if you choose to display your obsession with the South Indian mrdangam music you've recently been listening to, cool. Just don't expect to get the gig.

Bring the right colors. In LA, this usually means bright colors or pastels. In New York, it's black, black, black. (Yes, I'm kidding! I'm talking about sonic color!) If you're bringing gear to the audition, make sure it fits the sonic color of the music you're going to play. Loud rock band? Bring some loud rock band cymbals, not those vintage Ks. If you're playing on equipment that is supplied by the club, church, band, or rehearsal studio, then quickly try to adjust the tone of the drums to what you've been hearing on the audition tape or CD.

"Money is always the tricky issue, isn't it? In my opinion, it's not appropriate to talk about money until **after** they want you."

Time wars. This one's a bit tricky. Let's say you're auditioning, but the bass player is *slowing down*. He's already got the gig, you don't. Are you supposed to allow that to happen? To what degree do you keep the time? This scenario actually happened to me last week. Well, in this case, I just played the darned music. I gently kept the tempo where I thought it should be and hoped that they were taping the audition. (I'm hoping they later said, "Wow, Billy really held it together, didn't he?" Ha!)

By the way, I didn't get this particular gig. But I believe it happened because I hadn't convinced myself that I truly wanted the gig. (See above.) It wasn't a style of music that I could love. (Next week I'm going to hate myself for this.) But play the best you can—*period*. That includes nailing the time, dynamics, and groove as best you can, no matter who else is in the room.

Ooh, ooh, ooh...fashion! (I'm talking about hair, pants size, and even your *race*.) A guitarist friend of mine couldn't audition with popular singer/actress "X" until a picture was taken, to make sure that his hair was long enough. I think this used to be more common in the '70s and '80s. Hair and pants size were very important factors in getting a gig back then.

I don't frown on the fact that some music is sold assisted by what's considered good looks. At least it's getting sold. For all I know, Mozart had all kinds of weird problems with his kings or benefactors like we have with clubs and record labels.

Lately, I'm happy to see some interesting looking people of more diverse shapes and sizes on album covers and in videos. There will always be some people that just won't hire you because they don't like the way you look. We rejected ones just have to get over it.

There will always be bad audition experiences. Some things are never going to change. Don't make the mistake of thinking that your own personal bad audition stories are unique to you. And don't ever imagine that there will be a day when you don't have to go through this kind of horror.

Now it's *payback time*. The following story is from my own personal experience. The names have been changed to protect the guilty. But hopefully, they'll know who they are!

A few years back, I auditioned for a big pop star, "Benny Woodens" I'll call him. Well, at my audition, a chiropractor came in and set up a portable table and proceeded to work on "Benny" right in front of my *&%@% bass drum—*while* I was playing. Then, at the end of my audition, Benny was too busy to talk to me because he was concentrating on his plate of sushi. Yes, it was in LA. No, I didn't get the gig. But that's auditioning for ya!

•

Chapter 16

Hi-Hats Are The **Best**!

Options & Exercises

I see the modern drumset as an orchestra. Toms are like a stabbing horn section. Cymbals are violins—and sometimes they are *violence*. But this particular article is more about independence and how we incorporate the four things that we do at once. Assuming each of us has four limbs playing the drums, why not look at the drumset as a four-piece percussion ensemble?

When I "compose" a drum track for a song, I like to make sure that each instrument introduced into the song has a full life throughout the song. An example? Well, let's say the tune starts off at a medium-soft volume, and some simple time is happening—cross-stick on the snare, for instance. Now, when that cross-stick escalates into a full-on backbeat, the "cow is out of the barn," right? It's going to stay there for the rest of the song, unless the softer dynamic is re-installed, like maybe in

the bridge or a re-intro to another verse.

I'll start playing a song like this, trying all kinds of things—hands, mallets, all kinds of complex stuff—but then after a few takes, I'll narrow it down and get to the simplest part, the essence of what the drums should be doing. This brings us to one of the "big four elements" of the drumset, one member of that percussion ensemble I mentioned earlier—the hi-hat.

My use of the hi-hat is one of the most personal things I do as a drummer. I have a fixation—you might say an obsession—with the hi-hat. It is *so* underrated and underused in a musical way by so many drummers, and it is such an essential part of my playing.

In jazz, there are many examples of creative uses of the hi-hat. Tony Williams, Papa Jo Jones, Elvin Jones...hell, *all* those guys saw the hats as an essential musical accent device to the rhythmic fabric of their groove.

Let's go back to that pop track with the medium-soft first verse. Let's say the hat is playing 8th notes, and there's a cross-stick on 2 and 4. When the dynamics get bigger, the snare comes in and the hat keeps going. Then there's the chorus of the song (or certainly the bridge), and the drummer goes to the ride cymbal (maybe the bell). What's up with the hi-hat? It's been the chunky 8th-note rhythm foundation up 'til now, and when the drummer goes to the ride, it *disappears*.

Most drummers have the hat follow the snare on 2 and 4 (with their left foot) at this point, because it's convenient to have that side of the body in unison. There are guys who can do *amazing* things on drums with their feet and hands who don't have good independence with their hi-hat. Admittedly, sometimes after all that crunchy 8th-note action, a more open feel is desired, and the hi-hat needs to take a rest. But many times there's a need to keep that 8th-note energy happening.

If a guitar player is playing 8th notes in that section, then he's taken over the hi-hat part. But if the space is there and the need is there, why doesn't the hi-hat keep ticking? It just takes a little practice. Are you able to *choose* what happens with one-fourth of your drum ensemble?

And are you basing that choice on sound or convenience?

Here are a few exercises that might open up some hi-hat independence for you. I could give you enough hi-hat exercises to fill an entire book, but I'd rather have you take these few examples and build on them yourself. Make up your own personal hi-hat challenges, and base your made-up exercises on a musical purpose. Keep your ears *open* in the practice room.

Here's a simple beat, much like the one mentioned above, only with a 16th-note pattern on the hi-hat.

Now, to give that hi-hat its own life, mix in some foot chicks, instead of using only sticks on the hat. This adds a whole world of dynamics to the groove. (Be sure that the stick hits are on a *closed* hi-hat. You want to develop the control to be able to play a "chick" sound on the hats with your foot and then immediately play a closed hat with your stick, or vice versa. This may be hard to do in the beginning.)

2

Also, as a variation, try this:

3

On the example above, I tend to come down with the right hand on the first 16th, as well as drop the foot. This succeeds in adding yet another subtle color to the sound. Also, I'll likely accent a bit with the right hand, like this:

4

A subtle variation to this involves not playing the hat when the snare is playing. This adds a special lilt to the groove.

5

I love being able to open the hat just a bit before it closes with the foot, for a little bit of "pea soup" (as it sounds), or maybe it's just a little "pist" sound.

6

Notice that *none* of the hits before the foot hits are open. It's easier to play them open, but it's *great* to learn to control the choice of open or closed. Work on being able to choose just how much the hat is open in these situations. Get detailed and subtle control over this, and your grooves will get deeper and deeper.

On top of all this, try some of these with different bass drum patterns. Try some patterns with more than just 1 and 3 on the bass drum. Here's a very simple idea for a change in the bass drum.

7

Once you "own" these suggested patterns, you'll probably start coming up with your own possibilities. It might seem hard to master these concepts at first. But eventually you'll receive a greater balance on the kit. Both of your feet will be involved in the grooves you play (and that adds up to more mechanisms). Also, your entire *body* will be involved in the groove. That will make it easier for you to lock in your tempos.

More **Options** For Hi-Hats

Many drummers, when they play the ride cymbal, allow their left foot on the hi-hat to blindly follow the snare drum—2...4...2...4...bor...ing...*bor...ing*! It ends up sounding like the hi-hat is that little brother you had when you were nine years old who wanted to follow you everywhere—the one you were trying to ditch! Get the picture?

I like to see each drum and cymbal on my kit as a character in a movie. Each character in my "groove movies" must have a full and interesting life. To make each voice of the kit full and interesting, I need to have control over many different dynamics and sounds for each voice, *including the hi-hat*. We scratched the surface of what you can do with your hi-hat in my last article. But here are a few more ways that I give the hi-hat some life.

Let's stay in 16th-note land, and let's say you're playing a song with your band and are about to go to the ride cymbal for the bridge.

But, to me, playing 16th notes on the ride can get too ringy. Here's an idea that implies the 16th feel with your hi-hat foot without the sound getting too ringy. (I think of this as just a little "skip" on the hat before the snare backbeat.) By the way, the right hand on the ride is alternating between the bell (on downbeats, indicated with a dot above the note) and the shoulder area of the cymbal.

Now I'll add some "ghost notes" (kind of an acoustic digital delay) on the snare to extend the 16th-note feel even more. This one might take some time for you to accomplish. Start slowly and get comfortable with the hi-hat part with the ride before you add the snare ghost notes.

Paul La Raia

Any instrument can imply the 16th-note vibe. The following example involves the bass drum and a slight shift in the hi-hat pattern to the "&" of 2 and 4.

In the next example, your left stick moves back and forth between the snare drum and hi-hat, adding even more meat to the groove.

Once these ideas become comfortable for you, the hi-hat will be involved on an equal level on the kit. You'll feel a wonderful flow with your body as you play your grooves. And when this stuff is *truly* comfy for you, you'll be able to groove with the left hand, left foot, and bass drum *alone*. This will free up your right hand for painting colors on the cymbals while the left side is taking care of business, or in my case, picking up that stick I just dropped!

Chapter 18

Sound Ideas

Want more sounds out of your drum-ming? Here's some ideas to keep in mind. Try to get comfortable with these playing tools:

Wire (jazz) brushes.

For inspiration, listen to Jim Keltner play brushes, or Papa Jo Jones, or try the early '60s Bill Evans jazz piano trio records with Marty Morrell or Paul Motian on drums. Can you do this with brushes…or can you at least incorporate *some* of it into your playing?

Various sizes of wooden rods and plastic versions of rod-type brushes and all their differing thicknesses.

The difference in sound between the sizes and types of various drumming "utensils" are critical in recording. Microphones really hear a difference with the different thicknesses.

Sticks: Do you prefer wood or plastic tip?

A plastic tip might be better to get a more focused "ping" out of thinner cymbals. Also, have you experimented enough with your stick size and weight?

Try playing the drums with your hands.

It's fun!

Get comfortable playing with shakers.

For starters, instead of a hi-hat pattern, or instead of holding a stick in your right hand (for righties), hold a shaker and play the hat with the shaker!

Try taping a shaker to a stick or a rod-type stick.

The weight shift makes it harder to play. It takes some time to get used to this, but it sounds *wonderful*. It's like adding a percus-sionist to the band.

Paul La Raia

"Keep looking for **new ways** to get interesting colors out of whatever is in your hand."

And try the following checklist:

Keep looking for **new ways** to get interesting colors out of whatever is in your hand, and acquire the technique to get that sound. Find and develop grooves with your newfound shaker/brush skills. Encourage sonic nuance (subtlety).

Notice how to get **different pitches** from cross-sticks...and practice being able to choose and manipulate them. Where you place the stick across the hoop will change the pitch of the cross-stick sound. Also, whether the snares are on or off changes things. Plus, can you play cross-sticks without muffling the snare head so it rings when hit?

Are you willing (and able) to decide **which cymbal** you ride or crash, based on its pitch? Some cymbals really stand out on certain songs because of their pitch.

How many sounds can you get out of a hi-hat? Does pressure from your closed foot affect the pitch of the hi-hat? For some cymbals, yes. How about yours?

Learn **the pitches** of your drums and your cymbals. Then notice how they interact with each other. Do some of your cymbals have a similar pitch to one of your toms? Or do they at least sound like they're in the "same key"?

Do your **cymbals have pitches** between them that are similar to the intervals of your drums? Fills can be played *on cymbals* as well as toms. Also, a ride pattern usually played on a cymbal can be played on a tom.

From now on, use part of a rehearsal with your band to determine **which cymbal sounds best** in that chorus, and, of course, which tom or toms to use on that fill—*or* backbeat.

In the studio, take it a step further and see which snare drum sounds best for the pitch and attitude of the song. Also, which bass drum? And do you really want all those toms on that particular track?

Try to see **how many sounds you can get out of one drum**—and play solos applying this technique to all of your drums.

Can you play a **solo based more on pitch** than varying rhythms? Try it and develop your ideas. It might open some new things up for you.

The way that you tune your drums should and will affect the way you play. So feel free to change the way they sound (or are set up) depending on your gig or mood. This is a great way to get out of those "practice doldrums" and find some new tuning and playing techniques!

For example, I always become more of a reggae drummer if the drums are all taped up, compared to wide open. Another example: If the snare is pitched really high, I tend to want to play some scorching hip-hop kind of thang.

Instead of tuning your toms as a section (all with a similar sound, with just a differing pitch), try **tuning your toms to extreme places**, so that one has absolutely nothing to do with the next. And start playing and making music with them.

For example, make your first tom sound like a timbale, the second extremely muffled, and the third as low as it will possibly go. This is yet another way to shake things up in your practice routine (especially if you follow certain patterns pretty regularly).

Always record yourself when you play with people, and check your feel, time, and *tone*. In other words, put yourself through what you've just put your bandmates through. Imagine being the bass player or guitarist and having to deal with *you* as a drummer.

And finally, **personalize your technique**. *Art lies in the details*. Technique isn't just speed, it can be more about your ear's skills. Great bands don't choose their drummer based on how fast he can play. I believe it's more important to be the kind of drummer who, when the guitarist and bassist are playing with you, they feel safe, confident, and inspired.

•

Chapter 19

Billy's **Quickie** Chart System

When I'm called to do a session or rehearsal, I sometimes find it hard to remember all of the music I'm presented with, especially if I'm working a lot. Sometimes I'll find myself playing in several different situations in the same week! I've found that having the ability to create a quick, condensed, and accurate "road map" of a piece of music is extremely helpful. I've come up with some short cuts for writing these "quickie" charts that may be of help to you.

By using the following system, I'm able to take an involved piece, even a fourteen-page drum chart (something I recently had to do on a session for George Russell), and condense it down to four pages. That means fewer page turns! Of course, most of us play music that's primarily about feel, where not too much detail is needed. But this system is very helpful in that setting as well.

Your Basic Chart

Sure, most of us freelance drummers write "cheat sheets." Some people I know write them on index cards; I sometimes write them directly on my snare head! But most quickie charts basically cover the form of the song—how it starts, what happens in the middle, how it ends. But I like to add a few other items.

At the top of my charts I'll sometimes write the title of another song I know that has a similar tempo, groove, and—most importantly—*attitude*. I also write down a drummer's name to help me zero in on that attitude. For example, if the song has a really big, powerful, open-rock feel, I might write "Bonham." If the song is a sexy R&B tune with lots of ghost notes, I'll write "Purdie."

If there are predetermined fills that I need to play, I'll put a squiggle where they happen and trust myself to play a fill that fits the song. If the songwriter wants a *specific* fill, I write it out. Then there's no mistake.

CNO
1M6
VERSE
VOCAL
MINI-DISK!
WHY CANT WE LIVE Together 104
"Do Do Doos"
C.S. - Left
Brush - Rt
SMILING FACES (Lickin Stick)
STICKS
ST.T. - SWANG
NO HAT TRICK!
SHKR
STK.
Weight 78
LOVES IN ME TODAY
START FF (Petty)
SHKR
STK
95
WIRE
I'll Be AROUND 98
BRUSH (SM OFF)
KICK ON ONE
"STAR"
HSBC
ENTERTAINMENT PARTNERS
JAGGED
FILL
Lick
HARD

True To Form

All popular music I've encountered has somewhat consistent qualities. There's usually an intro (sometimes called a "vamp") at the beginning, followed by a verse, and eventually what some people call the "refrain" or "chorus." Sometimes there's a bridge in the middle. In jazz or other perhaps "harder to peg" music, musicians title each section with a letter, like so: A = verse; B = refrain or chorus; C = bridge; D = another new section. This basic system works and is very easy to understand.

Now that you understand the basic form found in most simple charts, here are the abbreviations *I* use for the different sections of tunes:

1. INTRO = The opening section of a tune.

2. VAMP = Where the rhythm section repeats chord changes at the beginning of (or after) any section.

3. V1 = This indicates the first verse. Subsequent verses would be notated as V2, V3...you get the idea.

4. PRE = I call the section that *usually* follows the verse the "pre-chorus," because it always builds to the chorus.

5. CHO = This indicates the chorus.

6. BDG = If there's a bridge, this is how I label it.

7. I use a couple of different markings for solos. If a solo is over the verse chord changes, I name the instrument soloing and the section of the solo. For example, a keyboard solo played over verse chord changes would be notated KYBD V. If there's a guitar solo played over chorus changes, I write GTR CHO.

8. After all this stuff has happened, there's either a fade ending or a real ending. If it's a fade ending over a repeating chorus, I'll write CHO FADE. If the song has a real ending, I'll write OUTRO.

One other pointer about writing out the form: If I have the time, I'll use two different color highlighting pens to mark the choruses and the pre-choruses. That makes it very easy to see where I'm at in the chart.

Samples

Let's look at a couple of examples to see how easy this system actually is. This first chart is the one I used for the song "Devaney's Goat/The Whistling Postman," which is the duet I played with John Patitucci on my album, *Two Hands Clapping*. You can easily see the form (letters), the length of the sections by measure (numbers written below the letters), and the styles and solos that occur.

To give you an idea of how this works with a song you might be familiar with, I wrote out a quickie chart for the Joan Osborne hit "(What If God Was) One Of Us?" It only took me two listens to write it, and now I can sit down and play the song without a problem.

At the top of the chart I wrote the basic beat of the tune. The attitude is addressed: "Take Your Time, Big Guy!" tells me to play with an open and relaxed feel. I mentioned earlier that the squiggles indicate fills, and you'll see them in a few spots here. The "flags" (looking a bit like check marks) indicate cymbal crashes. The "C.S." in the last line is how I indicate cross-stick.

The very process of taking the time to write out a chart helps my easily distracted mind remember the songs. At the beginning of a new gig, charts are indispensable. I feel more confident and play better with them. And the best part of all of this is, when you nail the arrangement and lay down a solid performance, your bandmates think you're a genius!

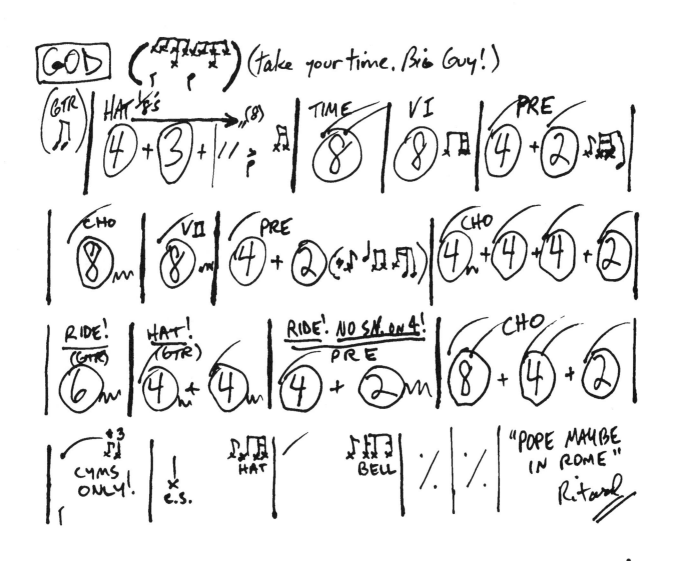

Billy On **Record**

These are the records that Billy says best represent his drumming:

Artist	Album
Billy Ward	Two Hands Clapping
Bill Champlin	He Started To Sing
Robbie Robertson	Storyville
The Knack	Serious Fun
Jim Beard	Lost At The Carnival
Jim Beard	Truly
Carly Simon	Film Noir
George Russell	It's About Time
	Under Siege (film soundtrack)
	That Thing You Do (film soundtrack)

…and here are a few that he listens to for inspiration:

Artist	Album	Drummer
Tom Waits	Bone Machine	Brain, Tom Waits
Beatles	any	Ringo Starr
Jimi Hendrix	any	Mitch Mitchell, Buddy Miles
James Brown	any	Clyde Stubblefield, Jabo Starks
Miles Davis	any	Tony Williams, Jimmy Cobb, Al Foster, etc.
The Band	Music From Big Pink	Levon Helm
Cat Stevens	Greatest Hits	Gerry Conway, Harvey Burns

Billy's Favorite Drummers

Meat 'n' potatoes = Art Blakey and John Bonham

Tasteful = Ringo Starr and Papa Jo Jones

Groovin' = Jeff Porcaro and Mel Lewis

Fire = Keith Moon and Elvin Jones

Wonderfully surprising = Paul Motian and Joey Baron

Funky = Zigaboo Modeliste and Bernard Purdie

Favorite rock ballad fills = Nigel Olsson

Unbelievable chops = Terry Bozzio and Vinnie Colaiuta

Down-home and creative = Levon Helm and Jim Keltner

Versatile and always great = Steve Gadd

For more fun "Ward-isms," drumming tips and thoughts, and the place to go to order Billy's album, *Two Hands Clapping*, check out his Web site at www.billyward.com.